The Good Prison Off

This book offers a solution-focused and strengths-based guide to becoming an effective Prison Officer. Written and developed by a collection of ex-prisoners who are all now professionals, practitioners, and educators in the criminal justice field, the book draws on lived experience and the diverse literature on prisons and penal policy to explore good and bad examples of professional practice.

The book is informed by the belief that those with direct experiences of custody and incarceration offer a vital perspective on the efficacy of penal practice. While these voices are often accessed through research, it is rare they are seeking to lead the conversation. This book seeks to reset this balance. Drawing on themes such as discretion, respect, relationships, and legitimacy, it offers recommendations for best practices in developing a rehabilitative culture in prison.

This book will be of interest to practitioners, researchers, and educators alike. It is essential reading for all those engaged with prisons, punishment, penal practice, desistance, and rehabilitation.

Andi Brierley is a University Teacher at Leeds Trinity University (LTU), delivering the Unlocked MSc in Applied Custodial Leadership in partnership with the Unlocked Graduates.

'This is a powerful, original, and deeply moving account of the best kinds of work that prison officers can do and the life-changing impacts of that work. It is written collaboratively, and with passion and insight, by a 'redemption community' – professional wounded healers – who have lived experience of adult and children's prisons. It is such a positive and inspiring contribution - every prison officer should read it.'

Alison Liebling, *Institute of Criminology, Cambridge*

'This highly engaging and original collection provides crucial insight into the various ways that prison officers can shape the experience of imprisonment through forms of relational investment. Conveying tumultuous backgrounds and complex interior lives, it illuminates how seemingly minor acts of humanity and inhumanity, or dismissiveness and support, can change a prisoner's orientation to his or her sentence and set the course for a different future'

Ben Crewe, *Professor of Penology and Criminal Justice and Deputy Director of the Prisons Research Centre*

'This book's simple proposition is that any attempt to improve prisons must involve careful listening to the voices of people that live or have lived inside them. More specifically: If you want to know how the everyday exercise of penal power can avoid harm and maybe even do some good, then you ★must★ listen to people who have been on its receiving end. For as long as prisons persist, I hope those who work in or study prisons, and who make penal policy, will read this book. It is jam-packed full of such hard-earned wisdom and compassion. It is deeply thoughtful and powerfully affecting, constructive and challenging, critical and practical. Please read it — and ponder the human potential that we might release if we could radically rethink our approaches to punishment.'

Fergus McNeill, *Professor of Criminology & Social Work at the University of Glasgow*

'This book is innovative and very informative. As a former Prison Officer, myself, it was sadly often the case that we did not see the successes that can happen. The accounts in this book are inspirational from the authors showing that indeed many prisoners go on to change their lives and undeniably payback tenfold to a system that needs careful consideration and change. In this respect it provides a sense of hope that is sadly often lacking within our prison systems. It was heart-warming to read the gratitude in these pages and that on occasions Prison Officers do get it right in the realms of undertaking an often difficult and thankless task. This book does not raise security concerns, it is not ex-prisoners telling Prison Officers how to do their job properly, moreover it is an honest and open account of the power that positivistic relationships can have to help overcome adversity if small adjustments are made. In my opinion it is a must read for any Prison Officer and indeed anyone who wants to explore the complex power of relationships taking place within the carceral space.'

Russell Woodfield, *Lecturer in Forensic Psychology and Criminology*

The Good Prison Officer

Inside Perspectives

Edited by Andi Brierley

Routledge
Taylor & Francis Group

LONDON AND NEW YORK

Designed cover image: © Shutterstock Pavlo Lys

First published 2023
by Routledge
4 Park Square, Milton Park, Abingdon, Oxon OX14 4RN

and by Routledge
605 Third Avenue, New York, NY 10158

Routledge is an imprint of the Taylor & Francis Group, an informa business

ISBN: 978-1-032-39439-8 (hbk)
ISBN: 978-1-032-39440-4 (pbk)
ISBN: 978-1-003-34974-7 (ebk)

DOI: 10.4324/9781003349747

Typeset in Bembo
by KnowledgeWorks Global Ltd.

Contents

Contributors

Andi Brierley is a Senior University Teacher at Leeds Trinity University, former Youth Justice Specialist, and Author of crime and justice books from a lived experience and practice perspective.

Kevin Neary is the Co-Founder of Aid&Abet in Scotland and Recovery Practitioner using his lived experience to support prison leavers and creating opportunities for employment.

Max Dennehy is a Housing Support Worker and Criminology Student at Lancaster university using his recovery pathways to guide others into recovery.

Kierra Myles is a Mentor Coordinator for the Government of Jersey using her lived experience to provide mentorships for others with lived experience.

Daniel Whyte is a Co-Director of Doing What Really Matters (DWRM) Consultants and University Lecturer – using his life sentence to provide education for other prisoners.

Devon Ferns is an Early Help Support Worker for Rotherham's Youth Justice Service and Participation Lead using his lived experience to support children co-design their interventions.

James Docherty is a Violence Reduction Officer in Scotland and Advisor at Community Justice Scotland which places prevention at the heart of social justice.

Disclaimer

The views from myself and every contributor to this book are our own personal experiences and perspectives of our journeys through the prison system. They do not in any way represent our employees or the institutions we work for or with. We recognise and acknowledge that these experiences and views may be inclusive of others that may not have provided permission for their use. This has been considered from the start and every step of the journey has ensured we have mitigated this through confidentiality steps as much as possible or obtained permission.

Acknowledgements

This book is a coming together of what can only be described as a wonderful team of souls that have experienced some challenging times. These chapters are a demonstration of their humanity, commitment, and dedication. Several kind human beings that simply want to improve the prison system they have first-hand experience. Simultaneously improving the experiences of those that enter the justice system as well as those that work in it, reducing victims in the process. It is for this reason that I want to acknowledge that this wouldn't have been possible without Max Dennehy, Daniel Whyte, Kevin Neary, Devon Ferns, James Docherty and Kierra Myles Not to mention Shadd Maruna who has always advocated for learning from those with experience of the justice system and Fritzi Horstman for bringing her unique international perspective of working in US prisons to the project. Last but by no means least, the endorsers Professor Ben Crewe, Professor Fergus McNeill, Dr Russ Woodfield and Professor Alison Liebling for their wonderful endorsements.

Andi Brierley – October 2022

Foreword

This book is both remarkable and unprecedented. Indeed, the most remarkable thing about it might be that it is unprecedented. The premise behind this collection is manifestly sensible that it is hard to believe that no one has ever produced a book like it. If you wanted to know what makes a great lecturer, you need to ask students who listen regularly to lecturers. If you wanted to know what makes a great customer service representative, you need to listen to customers. The logic could not be more simple. Yet, no one, to my knowledge has ever collected the wisdom of the formerly incarcerated to better understand what makes a good prison officer before this fantastic collection.

What on earth could explain this? Perhaps, the explanation can be found in the nature of prison work. Unlike almost any of the cognate occupations – nursing, social work, social care – prison work is not taken seriously as a professional career. The work that the prison officer is expected to do is incredibly complex, multifaceted, and valuable to wider society. At a minimum, officers are expected to have a level of expertise about suicide, self-harm, violence, bullying, drug use, addiction, race relations, mental health, nutrition, medication, exercise, and something called rehabilitation. Yet, the levels of training and education required to be employed in these extraordinarily difficult workplaces is usually as minimal and insulting as the starting salaries. Just as importantly, the goals of prison work are not clear. One can hardly become a 'good prison officer' if it is unclear what prison officers are supposed to be doing. Are they there to punish people? To prevent any escapes? To 'manage' and 'control' the unruly? For many of us, it is clear that prison work is far less about security than it is about helping people. It is a social service career requiring a considerable amount of people skills (far beyond physical constraint or intimidation) only without the education or respect given to those in equivalent 'helping professions'.

On the other hand, perhaps the explanation has more to do with the experts on display here. In almost every other social service, from patient care in hospitals to students in a university, the value of consulting end users has long been taken for granted. These "experts by experience" have insights that cannot be learned in a textbook or a secondary data analysis. The only logical way to improve service delivery is to consult those for whom the services are targeted. Yet, this almost axiomatic insight seems to have largely bypassed the world of prisons, where service delivery is in absolutely desperate need of improvement. Surely, this is partially because the people in prison are distrusted, discredited, and perceived to be manipulators and complainers.

As a result, we have an almost perfect storm of non-accountability. Prison work is a helping profession that is not judged by the help it gives and does not consult the recipients of this help in seeking to improve it. This fascinating book, then, represents an invaluable first step on the road toward normalisation, professionalism, and progress in prison work. It might be too extreme to say that no one should be allowed to wear the uniform of the prison officer before they have read these chapters. Yet, it is certainly the case that it would be extremely difficult to become a "good" prison officer without listening to the wisdom of lived experience.

Shadd Maruna, Professor of Criminology and advocate of prisoner's voice.

Preface

The thinking behind this book is one of inclusion, equality, collaboration, redemption, and community. As a University Teacher at Leeds Trinity University, teaching prison officers on the Unlocked Graduates MSc Scheme, it struck me that there is a lack of prisoner narratives within prison and prison officer literature. Having been in prison and spent years receiving criminal justice services before I officially left school, I know all too well that theory, practice, and reality do not always complement each other. If students from fields such as criminology, sociology, etc. want a full picture, then inside perspectives of prison and lived experience narratives are essential to learn and unpick.

The easiest element of creating a project like this was finding like-minded people that had been to prison, now professionals that; a) believe the prison service needs help, and b) would be willing to offer themselves to help create a better prison service. The team were all selected because they had lived experience of being in care as children, being excluded from school, youth incarceration and chronic addiction. This was because like me, the authors have faced significant social barriers before experiencing incarceration. It is therefore important to hear the voices and narratives of these individuals. Many ex-prisoners that were successful before prison often come out and have their views on prisons heard. It is the marginalised and excluded that are often forgotten. Most prison books are written by professionals that worked in them or by academics that research them. This was the driver for the book, and the selection of those that co-authored the book with me. Plain sailing then I hear you say? Not quite.

After approaching the team and agreeing dates for completion of the chapters, I thought the same. 'It is simple this editing stuff, Andi' I almost convinced myself back in January 2022 when we all agreed to the project. Because the book is about lived experience and how certain people are excluded from practice, policy and literature, every decision will be made together, collaboratively with co-production in mind. 'Very considerate and inclusive, Andi' I again told myself, patting myself on the back. However, as a university teacher, why on earth I thought because I had provided submission deadlines, that a group of busy professionals were going to stick to them, I will never know. Hindsight is everything, but I certainly should have given them all 5-day extensions.

Furthermore, giving equal weight to the decision-making processes to a very passionate group of people that have experienced prison also brought its own unique challenges. Inclusion is great; however, it often doesn't happen because it can be hard work. After obtaining Routledge as a publisher due to sending out the book proposal to various publishers seemed like a milestone for a group of ex-prisoners, regardless of us all being in professional roles. None of us are doctorates just yet (not yet Dan Whyte). So, the questions from the team to keep them up to date on contract agreements, book launch ideas and which charity to give the royalties to were certainly not straight forward. Having said all that, this journey has developed friendships along the way. Smiles and giggles in the WhatsApp Group titled The Good Prison Officer, occupied by a group of ex-prisoners. Imagine!

I am very proud to have been a part of this journey with not just colleagues or co-authors, but with friends. For anyone that doesn't yet understand what 'redemption communities' mean, this is exactly it. Yes, after being in prison, we as ex-prisoners need to be accepted as equals to our none prison experienced community members to achieve the tertiary stage of desistance. However, we often find solace and acceptance in the friendships of others that have taken the desistance journey, and this book is evidence of that sense of community and acceptance. Take this journey with us. Feel the solidarity within the pages. The authenticity of real-life stories with no pre bias, other than to make the prison system better for prisoners, officers, victims, and every soul that is touched in one way or another by the prison system.

Abbreviations

ACE	Adverse Childhood Experience
CAHMS	Children and Adolescent Mental Health Services
CCE	Child Criminal Exploitation
CEO	Chief Executive Officer
CJA	Criminal Justice Alliance
CPP	Compassionate Prison Project
CPTSD	Complex Post Traumatic Stress Disorder
CSLA	Community Sport Leadership Award
DWRM	Doing What Really Matters
ETE	Education Training and Employment
FMI	Five Minute Interventions
HMIP	Her Majesties Inspectorate of Probation/Prison
HMP	Her Majesties Prison
HMPPS	Her Majesties Prison and Probation Service
IEP	Incentive and Earned Privileges
ILP	Independent Learning Plan
LE	Lived Experience
LTU	Leeds Trinity University
MACEs	Multiple Adverse Childhood Experiences
MI	Motivational Interviewing
MOJ	Ministry of Justice
NOMS	National Offender Management
PACT	Presence, Attunement, Connection and Trust
PO	Personal Officer
PO	Prison Officer
POELT	Prison Officer Entry Level Training
PRT	Prison Reform Trust
ROTL	Release on Temporary Licence
SMT	Senior Management Team

SO	Senior Officer
TF	CBT – Trauma Focussed Cognitive Behavioural Therapy
TWOC	Taking Without Owners Consent
VRU	Violence Reduction Unit
YCS	Youth Custody Service
YJS	Youth Justice System
YJW	Youth Justice Worker
YOI	Young Offenders Institution
YRO	Youth Rehabilitation Order

1 An Introduction to the Team and Project

Andi Brierley

The Driver for This Project

A recent study of reoffending rates conducted by the Ministry of Justice highlights that the estimated economic and social cost of reoffending in England and Wales stands at around £18.1bn (PFT, 2021). In 2021, the then Justice Secretary Domonic Raab stated that 'Prisons keep people safe by taking dangerous criminals off our streets, but they can only bring down crime and keep the public safer in the longer-term if they properly reform and rehabilitate offenders' (HMPPS, 2021 p.3). However, in contrast to that statement even the then Justice Secretary himself recognised in Her Majesties Prison and Probation Service (HMPPS) Prison Strategy White Paper that reoffending rates in England and Wales are 'stubbornly high' (HMPPS, 2021 p.7). Reoffending rates for those we do send to prisons here in England, Wales, and Scotland is one of the highest in Europe (Marsh et al., 2008). This is also true for the number of prisoners we send to prison per capita (Ryan & Ward, 2015). This leads us to question why then, if prison seems to be such an ineffective tool at reducing crime overall, are we using this punishment apparatus more than our European counterparts to address the issue of criminality? Moreover, where does the responsibility for the inadequacy lie?

There are many people, organisations, and services invested in making communities better by reducing reoffending rates and crime. Politicians want to be seen as being tough on crime. Victims want to see offenders and criminals being held to account – and potential victims want to know they live in safe communities. The public also wants to believe that the justice system can keep them safe and make sure offenders are deterred from crime. Judges, Barristers, Probation Officers, Youth Justice Officers, Police Officers, and of course Prison Officers want to reduce crime. They want to be good at their jobs, and to also make the difference many of them set out to make when

DOI: 10.4324/9781003349747-1

deciding their careers. However, one often forgotten group is those that have been convicted of crime. More specifically those that have been to prison themselves and that been directly impacted by the prison system because of their behaviour. As you navigate the chapters throughout this book, you will see many of these groups have their own drivers to improve the prison system. They often have axiomatic insights that can positively contribute to improving the prison system; whether in policy, practice or literature. Ex-prisoners often leave prison, but the experience of incarceration can leave a residue on their mind, body, and soul which has often been explained as post prison liminality (see Jewkes & Laws, 2021; John, 2017).

This book draws a group of ex-prisoners out of their liminal space and elevates their voices to lead the conservation on prison reform and challenge the notion of who writes the narratives. Providing inside prison perspectives from those with first-hand experience of the prison system itself. Prison is going to be used to respond to crime and in many cases within the status quo, the courts have limited options. However, this book aims to support the prison system to be more effective at reducing those stubbornly high reoffending statistics and create prison officer practice that can enhance transformational change and develop a positive prison culture. The authors of each chapter aim to achieve this through storytelling and sharing good practices through a unique lens of prisons in England, Jersey, and Scotland. To provide some context to the need for change, according to Ministry of Justice data on reoffending rates, between January to March 2020, 69.1% of Juveniles went onto commit a crime within 12 months of release; adults within this same period that served under 12 months were 57.5%; while for those serving over 12 months reoffending were 22.8% (MoJ, 2022). This context indicates that if we as the British public use prison more than our European neighbours, we need everyone to have an investment in improving these statistics. An improvement that ensures people that return to our communities from prison are less likely to re-offend than when they entered the prison system in the first place.

Breaking Down Barriers

People that leave prison often want to articulate how they were affected by the experience. I say this as I am indeed one of these individuals as we will find throughout the chapters of this book. Many of us that have experienced prison want to improve the justice system for people that we often identify with through a shared experience. Serving prisoners that many of us feel we have left behind. Some members of our group want to improve communities so that others do not experience the hardships we experienced. We have been described in scholarship as 'wounded healers' (LeBel 2007; Maruna, 2001; Maruna & Ramsden, 2004) or the 'professional ex' (Brown, 1991). Helping others heal from or avoid the social factors that have been argued to be the sociological reason many of us enter the system in the first place (Farrington et al., 2006). Prisoner to a wounded healer is a personal evolution that has been presented by leading criminologists to be a 'making good' process of reformation (Maruna, 2001). Reformed people with convictions, particularly those of us that have served time in prison often want to prove to ourselves and other people that we have moved on from offending in a practical and moral way. This is essentially the tertiary tenet of the desistance process (Graham & McNeill, 2017). Desistance is the theory of cessation of offending and changing one's identity from that of an offender; to a non-offender. Tertiary being the third stage is having one's new identity as a non-offending person or even pro-social self accepted by others in society, enabling one to develop a sense of trust from others - constructing the hope required for the transition to be understood and for us to be 'recognized as fellow human beings, and not just as offenders' (Ugelvik, 2022, p. 635).

As prisoners and ex-prisoners, we are often interviewed, researched, and have our lives transformed into data by those that require our perspectives in scholarship. This is of course due to the research being about us, and the evidence must be inclusive of our experiences to hold validation. This means we must be involved in one way or another. Furthermore, being interviewed by academics for research purposes inevitably turns into an interpretation of what has been said and then our narratives and perspectives are presented to others in ways we wouldn't necessarily present them. This can lead to a misrepresentation of narratives and perspectives, regardless of a rigorous methodology. With this in mind, the methodology and approach to this book is one of narrative sharing. In other words, allowing the authors to tell their stories and perspectives of their pathways into and out of crime, and how they experienced prison which holds true to *them*. Narrative Criminology indeed presents a way of understanding crime through studying storytelling and develops an understanding of how one experiences crime and desistance (see Sandberg & Ugelvik, 2016). Therefore, to authentically reach prison officers, those caught up in the justice system, and students, each chapter will have one structure for consistency purposes. The context and content will be decided by each author. These headings will be – who am I, my prison experience, and my advice from the inside.

There is a growing body of evidence that storytelling and experiential peer learning can also be effective in the desistance process and justice practice (see Buck 2018; Buck, 2020; Creaney 2020; Lenkens et al., 2021). When story and perspective sharing with many friends and the co-authors of this book with similar experiences of practice to myself, we find a commonality in thought amongst others that have gone from one side of the justice system to the other. That the employment of people with justice experience in justice organisations would be a positive step to service improvement. However, there seems to be very little attention paid to reducing the barriers that exist for this group in statutory services. Mike Nellis and Fergus McNeill identified this as a solution focussed approach to justice practice in their foreword to Allan Weavers (2008) autobiographical book. Weaver, an ex-prisoner turned Probation Officer himself stated he was discouraged in social work from using aspects of 'self' which could have been useful to demonstrate life beyond offending others. Indicating that the justice system is unsure of how to capitalise on lived experience individuals becoming professionals as this was an experience I wrote about through my own transition (Brierley, 2019). While we hear constant talk of a broken justice system and high reoffending rates, maybe this direct and authentic inclusion is a methodology to take a step in the right direction to take a truly inclusive approach. Demonstrating a progressive justice system, and an expansion of User Voice principles into practice and even academia (Barry et al., 2016).

As a team, we wanted to take this opportunity to break down some of the academic barriers to take a truly inclusive and participatory approach to prison and desistance literature. We have come together to take perspectives of people with lived experience of prison and desistance to those that work directly with others left in the prison system and provide academic insight for those that study both prisoners and prison itself. As a result, removing the interpretation to simply allow those with prison experience to express their perspectives of prison practice in their own constructive way. This approach is a collaboration that allows us to also make a difference in the day-to-day roles of prison officers and the system itself in a way that remains authentic to us. This book as the title suggests is about how to be *The Good Prison Officer*, from people that have experienced both good and bad prison practice. Not an interpretation by academics that have little experience of being a prison officer or a prisoner themselves. Not from inspectorates that regulate or inspect prisons and the day-to-day relationships between prisoners and officers, which are often very relational and productive as we will find. This project provides narratives directly from those of us that have experienced practice from officers while being serving prisoners. Those of us that have been touched in both positive and negative ways by the way prison officers have interacted with us on a day-to-day basis.

We find more lived experience mentors within charities or tokenistic speakers at conferences than academics or professionals within the statutory functions of the justice system. Given so many of us wish to give back, this may be an indication of the lack of value granted to experiencing prison, and the narratives that develop after reaching tertiary desistance. Jason Warr's wonderful chapter in the book 'Understanding Prison Staff' is one of few noted contributions to the literature. Yet this work demonstrates the real power of improving practice through story telling (Warr, 2008). Warr demonstrates the power of prison officer, prisoner relationships by explaining how officer Y challenged others on his behalf, leading to a much better experience of prison. However, there are not enough examples of this perspective that prison officers, students, and scholars can learn from within the literature. Again, creating a barrier between lived experience writing and audiences such as the lay justice worker, students, or potential justice employees. We know that real life stories (desistance) and scientific evaluations (what works) are both vital instruments because as it stands, we are some distance away from finding the formula to ceasing or preventing crime (see Maruna & Mann, 2019). Therefore, both require equal merit and validation within justice system practice and literature. This book is a collaboration that brings, practice, stories, and literature to the table to improve justice practice.

As the justice system attempts to change the identity or behaviour of prisoners, it should seek to include those that have made that very shift to be involved on an equal basis to enhance our chances of achieving this goal for others. This would seem a logical approach to take which would naturally develop more insight into how to go about achieving that goal. There is evidence to suggest that using this vantage point within criminal justice practice is in fact an effective approach to achieving desistance (Buck, 2020). Accepting that as with any justice initiatives, there are some identified limitations (see Buck, 2020; Wong & Horan, 2021). This book provides a unique prison insight in an accessible, first-hand, and authentic way through an exploration of intricate prison relationships and desistance, in combination of justice practice and literature. We as a team have challenged each other on this journey together to ensure each chapter is grounded in reflexivity, and not just biased subjective perspectives. Each chapter has been edited and everything has been done to be as objective as possible.

There are limitations of course when we explore lived experience narratives in terms of evidence. However, the insights are invaluable to the role of the prison officer, and we will conclude with recommendations for change to improve the prison system.

This book is written by a group of people that have a will and desire to break down some of these barriers and ensure lived experience voice contributes to prison officer practice. A voice that was recently described as the 'hushed, marginalized and silenced' on the matters of criminology (Lynch & Windle, 2021 p.1). Making this book a symbolic action of progress of not just asking prisoners their views for research purposes, but ex-prisoners becoming leaders of the conversation. This project is a collaboration of stories and advice for the prison system and prison officers that can enhance practice across the prison estate in several English-speaking countries. One must never forget that the justice system is a systemic function within a wider context of societal inequality (see Tyler, 2020). The machinery of inequality contributes to a certain stigma inscribed both internally and externally on those of us that have experienced prison which often impacts on how society values our perspectives (Moran, 2012). As a result of this point of reference of inequality, stigma, and alienation, although ex-prisoners have a wealth of knowledge and expertise, we are often not provided a seat at the policy or literature table so to speak. Not because of our convictions or any perceived risk. It is because we often developed internalised stigma, lack educational attainments, skills (at least acknowledged skills), and knowledge to articulate our points. Notwithstanding the lack of social networks to promote that voice, even if we eventually break free of the stigma and find it. Another blossoming tenet of this book is the collective and collaborative approach that developed friendships and networks along the journey. As history often illustrates, strength by numbers is an effective way to break down social barriers. As the lead author, I have been privileged to work alongside the team of dedicated humans. For some, this book is their first attempt at writing. We have all taken the journey together, supporting each other to and developing a sense of community and hope.

Professional Wounded Healers

It is important to stress that each chapter of this book is written by ex-prisoners that have obtained professional careers that can now articulate our personal experiences of prison, desistance, and our relationships with prison officers in a balanced, authentic, and solution focussed way. This dual perspective of experience and practice is a unique opportunity for participation and co-production. Lived experience and research are not adversarial but naturally compatible (Barnacle, 2004). Learners truly benefit from as many perspectives as possible to critique and draw their own conclusions. Prison officers are no exception. Shadd Maruna, a leading criminologist, and author of the foreword recently wrote a critical analysis of Narrative Criminology. He highlighted that criminology as a field is at risk of 'sinking into a set of cliques where criminologists read the work of others who think like them, write for those very same people and publish only in the journals that they and their colleagues are already reading' (Bosworth & Hoyle, 2011, p. 3; see also Maruna & Liem, 2021). Maruna was not pointing at lived experience inclusion per say. The point is a salient one and reiterates the need of inclusion of people on the outside of such 'cliques' that may have an alternative point of reference; and ways of expressing their narrative scripts (Maruna, 2001). Recovery scholars point to 'Alcohol Anonymous (AA) as a "powerful example" of how the process of giving back enhances the making good and desistance transition' (Best & Savic, 2014, p. 260). We as a team of prison experienced professionals have developed natural connections through this shared journey, demonstrating yet another powerful example of this collaborative point of collective social change.

In terms of diverse experiences of prisoners, I previously wrote a book about the perspective of children that experienced the justice system and interviewed three of those children when they became adults (Brierley, 2021). My previous book did not have a female voice. It did have a female contribution that needed to be withdrawn before publication which was disappointing. This book has a far more diverse input which does include the female voice. This is essential to provide the gendered viewpoint to the prison experience and ensure this book includes both male and female perspectives of prison and prison officer practice. We also have contributions from the Juvenile Estate, Young Offenders Institutions (YOI) as well as Adults. We have contributors that have many years in custody and others that served many short sentences. We have representations from minority prisoners, the care experienced, and ex-prisoners with drug and alcohol issues and recovery. Ensuring we were as inclusive as a project like this can be of the profile of many prisoners that are most likely to experience prison re-entry and the 'revolving door' (see Padfield & Maruna, 2006). After all, even men experience prison in different ways, so diversity is imperative to obtain the voices of the often excluded, even within an excluded group. Again, I reiterate that each author was selected because of their current practice experience, or in one way or another, being *professional* 'wounded healers.'

What Can We Achieve?

If we explore the central functions of what the role of a prison officer is according to the HMPPS, we find that although it is a multi-faceted role, it states that as a prison officer 'you will be responsible for supervising and managing prisoners decently, lawfully, safely and securely, ensuring that the routines of the prison operate effectively' (HMMPS, 2019). Therefore, the contributions within this book are a massive resource for aspiring prison officers, Criminology, and Sociology students, serving officers as well as those managing officers or creating policy and procedures that officers must follow. There will be experiences and tips for officers to use while being decent, lawful, and safe. Practical examples that can connect any justice professional to the lived realities of prisoners through heart-warming stories and tangible illustrations of what makes a difference to the lives of prisoners. Criminologists are now constructing theories of why people desist from crime, to enhance what we already know about why people commit crime (McNeill, 2012). This book, therefore, in a similar solution focussed way, transmits the learning prison officers obtain from those that continually return to prison through the 'revolving door' (Howerton et al., 2009), to those of us that desisted. Those of us that become professionals and how we put 'their' hard work into 'our' real life in practice.

The security part of the prison officer's role can be contributed to because of prisoner safety and relational practice. Maintaining a safe environment for prisoners is essential to relational work in prisons. However, the contributions and scope of this book are not going to meet all aspects of a prison officers' role such as security or risk management per say. This would be a step outside of the perspectives of all the contributing authors. Although several are currently working in roles where risk management is a central theme. This aside, when it comes to creating a rehabilitative culture, it is inevitable that those of us that have left crime and prison behind and gone on to make good through the desistance process can make a positive contribution. The stories and inside narratives of ex-prisoners creates an axiomatic knowledge of how prison officers can positively or negatively impact on the desistance process. These stories combined with literature from a wide range of disciplines from criminology to child development can influence practice and policy which creates a democratic approach within a co-production framework (Weaver, 2019). It is this rounded dual perspective that makes this book unique as well as an innovative contribution to the rehabilitation and desistance discourse.

Each contribution to this book aims to create 'Good Prison Officers,' or the officer Y in Jason Warr's chapter in 'Understanding Prison Staff' (Warr, 2008). We all came across them and acknowledge the more of them we have in prisons; the more likely we will be to create this so-called rehabilitative culture in prison that HMPPS strives for (Maruna & Mann, 2019). Prison officers are key to creating rehabilitative cultures. Yes, there are many factors outside of officer's controls that place strain on their day-to-day roles. We as prisoners understand them and the concluding chapter will present recommendations for change that if implemented will make officers work easier and is more likely to create a rehabilitative culture. Prison officers are vital to create safety in prisons. However, they require the support of stakeholders to achieve this very difficult task. Therefore, we as a team set out to ensure everyone cares more about the lived realities of the prison officers that are often described as the hidden heroes. Research into how COVID impacted prisons has found already strained relationships have further deteriorated (UserVoice, 2022). The inside perspectives from ex-prisoners for prison officers is one attempt at demonstrating how to rebuild and repair.

Hopefully, politicians and those leading on policy in positions of influence within the criminal justice system can take note of what is said about the power of relationships in a prison context and implement the concluding recommendations for change. We hope that as a result, the public and government understand the need for more investment to enhance the prison experience which will inevitably reduce victims when prisoners are released. That more resource is required within the prison estate to allow officers time, funding, and capacity to action what the inside perspectives outline in this book. That relationships make a difference when they are not placed under stress of an under resourced penal system that fails to live up to its own agenda (Ismail & de Viggiani, 2018). Although complex and challenging, this project and book is about trauma-informed principles within prison relationships, regardless of prison being a complex punitive sphere (Miller & Najavits, 2012). It is about community cohesion, compassion, empathy, and the restorative practice principles of working 'with,' not 'to' or 'for' prisoners (Finnis, 2021). Our book and project are about more than turning up to work and then going home. These chapters are about human contact and how powerful the role of the prison officer can be when officers lead with relational practice. Recognition that being a prison officer is a responsibility to everyone in the community, including but of course not only prisoners.

Within these chapters, you will find tips, techniques, real life examples of good practice, and tangible advice that can be utilised when working within a challenging environment with many prisoners identified as having complex needs (see Watson et al., 2004). Advice about how each author feels officers and others within the prison system contributed to our making good process. Our stories and voices are not coded and placed into themes through thematic analysis which can dilute and sanitise what we have to say. Our stories are not paragraphs of interviews which feed into reports for white papers or policies that are often not read by us as prisoners after contributing to them. Not lived experience contributions to intervention models that are constructed through the what works evaluations and put forward as effective because they are evidence based. These functions all play a vital role, and what works agenda is an instrumental tenet to developing better justice systems and services. None of the contributors would argue that education or project evaluations are not vital and imperative for learning and creating a more effective prison system. We are all aligned in the belief that if the prison system aspires to improve those stubbornly high reoffending rates, the lived experience stories, and voices of those that experience it first-hand need to be central to training and literature. Especially when presented with dual perspectives of lived experience and practice experience as is the case with every author in this book.

Lots of us that enter the prison system itself have experienced poverty, childhood trauma, been in care, addicted to drugs, spent time homeless and been excluded from school (Coates, 2017; Paton, 2009). The contributors to this work were handpicked due to their exposure to these social stressors prior to prison which make up a large proportion of the population. The social response seeking to address these issues should be to promote the voices of those with experiences of social stigma, poverty, and exclusion. Being convicted of a crime should not result in a refusal to listen to people that have indeed also been victims, long before they were perpetrators of an offence. Especially when the vantage point is of value. This is also an appropriate and fair social inclusion approach post prison. When we have served our time and desisted from crime, we should be free to make that positive contribution to justice practice and scholarship. Otherwise, what is the purpose of the sentencing procedures. This approach places equality of opportunity and desistance at the heart of every aspect of the criminal justice system. Inclusion of this perspective is the essence of participation, inclusion, co-production, and diversity.

Everyone, regardless of our social status, educational attainment, or employment title should be provided the opportunity to make a positive contribution to a public funded justice system, if they so wish. It is essential when we consider that the voices of those that enter the justice system that go on to desist from offending provide a source of knowledge and expertise to help those in the system help others to take that very journey. This seemed to be a fundamental point of Maruna's illustration of *Making Good* within the Liverpool Desistance Study (LDS) (Maruna, 2001). We have as much, if not more to learn from those of us that stop offending than we will from focusing our attention on those of us that do not. This is the spirit of this book, coproduction and participation at the heart of prison service literature. A book that is written, edited, and produced by ex-prisoner professionals with an intention of improving practice is a sign of progression, whichever way we look at it. Although there are many historical books by ex-prisoners, few have attempted to improve prison officer practice, or the prison system directly.

Therefore, when we consider what people with lived experience of prison bring in terms of developing better prison officers, we know that this vantage point can highlight what makes a good and bad prison officer from a unique perspective. A vantage point that has been previously neglected. This book brings that perspective to the table. If we are to reduce victims, if we are to make prisons safer places by attempting to create better relationships between prisoners and officers. It is simply very unlikely to be achieved if we continue to ignore the lived experience of prisoners. These voices aim to contribute alongside everyone else to create a better prison system that is positioned to help others deter from offending and follow our journeys out of crime to become positive contributors to society. After all, if this is not the aim of our very expensive prison system, then what is? The contributors and team in this book are doing this practically in our day-to-day lives. Our experience of incarceration and adversities prior to custody have become our greatest asset in doing so. We have now taken roles as leaders in our own communities, helping others less fortunate. Now we are here to share insight from our road to recover as a team of authors.

The Prison Officer

I have recently become a University Teacher, teaching prison officers that are new to the role on a graduate's scheme known as Unlocked Graduates. One of the most profound aspects of the experience is finding a lack of direct lived experience literature for the officers to learn from. The officers have occasional speakers that have experienced prison to listen to their stories shortly after leaving prison. This makes up such a small amount of the learning experience of the officers and is provided by lived experience with very little professional experience or knowledge. There seems no justifiable explanation as there are many lived experience contributors that return to the justice system after desisting from offending as professionals, even if this is mostly as mentors or within the charity or third sector organisations. Not that we need to continually talk about our personal experiences. I simply use my experiences to shape my front-line practice or how I teach what is in the literature as a teacher. Encouraging students to critique the literature in the same way my teaching colleagues do. One thing that I find interesting in teaching prison officers is the disconnect they claim between literature and practice. This would indicate a lack of prison officer operational contribution to the literature too.

I have however found a new sense of humanity in this new role teaching prison officers that I was not expecting when I was successful in interviews. I have come across so many wonderful humans that just want to make a positive difference to the lives of those in their prisons as prison officers. Often feeling unable to due to the lack of time, autonomy, and resource. This is fascinating for me as this was the case when I was first incarcerated as a child back in 1999. The driver for this book has come from bridging the gap between this lack of 'inside perspective' and supporting officers to better meet the needs of prisoners by having this handbook produced solely by ex-prisoners that is grounded in the day-to-day realities of prison life. Real life stories that can guide and advise those working with prisoners in prison and even in the community upon release. We as a team feel we can contribute to a much-needed morale boost as found by leading scholars in the field:

> 'If staff are not themselves treated decently and humanely, there will be little hope that they will apply such considerations in their dealings with prisoners' (Bennett et al., 2013 p. 242).

Prison officers and their roles have been misunderstood for some time as simply opening and closing doors and maintaining security by managing the risks within the prison walls (Arnold, 2016). A previously incarcerated scholar has explained that officers are as much a diverse population as prisoners. Even if few do live up to the stereotypes of 'bastards, failed coppers, or people that were bullied at school' (Warr, 2008, p. 17). This as we will see is not true and a misrepresentation of what many of us have witnessed on both sides of the justice fence. Many leading scholars have articulated that the role of prison officers is multifaceted and requires a great deal of skill now officers are expected to develop a rehabilitative culture whilst maintaining safety within prisons, which is no mean feat (Liebling et al., 2010). The role of prison officers is incredibly difficult because it has competing and sometimes conflicting roles that operate at varying levels. Not understanding this can lead to a misunderstanding of officers as 'power hungry enforcers of authority' (Arnold et al., 2012, p. 471).

It Is Not Us and Them, It Is 'We'

What this book aims to achieve is to ensure prison officers are provided with an insight that we believe, and even they claim is not freely accessible within the literature. Literature that is certainly not tangible and accessible for those prison officers that do not identify as academic or readily reach out to research-based reading. We will hopefully bring that literature to everyone in an accessible way. Through storytelling. We aim to ensure officers also know that we as ex-prisoners care about them and want them to do well. Not just because it will make them better at their jobs, increase public confidence, create safer communities, and reduce victims. Also, because we are all just humans and we must operate in spaces together, collectively as a community that provides hope and aspiration to the incarcerated. We can help, you can help others. If that is not the very essence of making good, giving back, and developing human connections through community cohesion, I am left wondering what making good is. We as a team aim to create connections and optimism through stories and inside perspectives to provide knowledge and skills for anyone working within the prison and justice system. Join us on this journey and you will find hope within every chapter.

References

Arnold, H. (2016). *The prison officer. Handbook on prisons* (pp. 265–283). Routledge.

Arnold, H., Liebling, A., & Tait, S. (2012). Prison officers and prison culture. In *Handbook on prisons* (pp. 501–525). Routledge.

Barnacle, R. (2004). Reflection on lived experience in educational research. *Educational Philosophy and Theory, 36*(1), 57–67.

Barry, M., Weaver, E., Liddle, M., Schmidt, B., Maruna, S., Meek, R., & Renshaw, J. (2016). Evaluation of the user voice prison and community councils. Final Report. https://strathprints.strath.ac.uk/65046/ Accessed 22/10/22.

Bennett, J., Crewe, B., & Wahidin, A. (Eds.). (2013. *Understanding prison staff.* Willan.

Best, D., & Savic, M. (2014). Substance abuse and offending: Pathways to recovery. In *Working within the forensic paradigm* (pp. 259–271). Routledge.

Bosworth, M., & Hoyle, C. (2011). What is criminology? An introduction. In M. Bosworth, & C. Hoyle (Eds.), *What is criminology?* (pp. 1–12). Oxford Univ. Press.

Brierley, A. (2019). *Your honour can I tell you my story*. Waterside Press.

Brierley, A. (2021). *Connecting with young people in trouble: Risk, relationships & lived experience*. Waterside Press.

Brown, J. D. (1991). The professional ex-: An alternative for exiting the deviant career. *Sociological Quarterly, 32*(2), 219–230.

Buck, G. (2018). The core conditions of peer mentoring. *Criminology & Criminal Justice, 18*(2), 190–206.

Buck, G. (2020). *Peer mentoring in criminal justice*. Routledge.

Coates, S. (2017). Unlocking potential: A review of prisoner education, Ministry of Justice, Dame Sally Coates, May 2016.

Creaney, S. (2020). Children's voices—are we listening? Progressing peer mentoring in the youth justice system. *Child Care in Practice, 26*(1), 22–37.

Farrington, D. P., Coid, J. W., Harnett, L., Jolliffe, D., Soteriou, N., Turner, R., & West, D. J. (2006). *Criminal careers up to age 50 and life success up to age 48: New findings from the Cambridge study in delinquent development (Vol. 94)*. Home Office Research, Development and Statistics Directorate.

Finnis, M. (2021). *Restorative practice*. Crown House Publishing Ltd.

Graham, H., & McNeill, F. (2017). Desistance: Envisioning futures. In P. Carlen & L. Ayres França (Eds.), Alternative criminologies (pp. 433–451). London: Routledge.

Her Majesties Prison and Probation Service (2021), Prisons strategy white paper, Retrieved 17 July 2022, from www.gov.uk.

Her Majesties Probation and Probation Service (2019), Prison Officer, Retrieved 27 March 2022, from (www.gov.uk.

Howerton, A., Burnett, R., Byng, R., & Campbell, J. (2009). The consolations of going back to prison: What 'revolving door' prisoners think of their prospects. *Journal of Offender Rehabilitation, 48*(5), 439–461.

Ismail, N., & de Viggiani, N. (2018). Challenges for prison governors and staff in implementing the healthy prisons agenda in English prisons. *Public Health, 162*, 91–97.

Jewkes, Y., & Laws, B. (2021). Liminality revisited: Mapping the emotional adaptations of women in carceral space. *Punishment & Society, 23*(3), 394–412.

Johns, D. F. (2017). *Being and becoming an ex-prisoner*. Routledge.

LeBel, T. P. (2007). An examination of the impact of formerly incarcerated persons helping others. *Journal of Offender Rehabilitation, 46*(1–2), 1–24.

Lenkens, M., Nagelhout, G. E., Schenk, L., Sentse, M., Severiens, S., Engbersen, G., & van Lenthe, F. J. (2021). 'I (really) know what you mean'. Mechanisms of experiential peer support for young people with criminal behavior: A qualitative study. *Journal of Crime and Justice, 44*(5), 535–552.

Liebling, A., Price, D., & Shefer, G. (2010). *The prison officer*. Willan.

Lynch, O., & Windle, J. (Eds.). (2021). *Giving voice to diversity in criminological research: 'nothing about us without us'*. Policy Press.

Marsh, K., & Fox, C. (2008). The benefit and cost of prison in the UK. The results of a model of lifetime re-offending. *Journal of Experimental Criminology, 4*(4), 403–423.

Maruna, S. (2001). *Making good* (p. 86). American Psychological Association.

Maruna, S., & Liem, M. (2021). Where is this story going? A critical analysis of the emerging field of narrative criminology. *Annual Review of Criminology, 4,* 125–146.

Maruna, S., & Mann, R. (2019). Reconciling 'desistance 'and 'what works'. *Academic Insights, 1,* 3–10.

Maruna, S., & Ramsden, D. (2004). Living to tell the tale: Redemption narratives, shame management, and offender rehabilitation. In A. Lieblich, D. P. McAdams, & R. Josselson (Eds.), Healing plots: The narrative basis of psychotherapy (pp. 129–149). American Psychological Association. doi: https://doi.org/10.1037/10682-007

Maycock, M., McGuckin, K., & Morrison, K. (2020). 'We are 'free range' prison officers', the experiences of Scottish prison service throughcare support officers working in custody and the community. *Probation Journal, 67*(4), 358–374. doi: https://doi.org/10.1177/0264550520954898.

McNeill, F. (2012). Four forms of 'offender' rehabilitation: Towards an interdisciplinary perspective. *Legal and Criminological Psychology, 17*(1), 18–36.

Miller, N. A., & Najavits, L. M. (2012). Creating trauma-informed correctional care: A balance of goals and environment. *European Journal of Psychotraumatology, 3*(1), 17246.

Ministry of Justice (2022). Proven reoffending statistics: January to March 2020. Retrieved 10 May 2022, from www.gov.uk

Moran, D. (2012). Prisoner reintegration and the stigma of prison time inscribed on the body. *Punishment & Society, 14*(5), 564–583.

Paton, J., Crouch, W., & Camic, P. (2009). Young offenders' experiences of traumatic life events: A qualitative investigation. *Clinical Child Psychology and Psychiatry,* 14(1), 43–62.

Padfield, N., & Maruna, S. (2006). The revolving door at the prison gate: Exploring the dramatic increase in recalls to prison. *Criminology & Criminal Justice, 6*(3), 329–352.

Ryan, M., & Ward, T. (2015). Prison abolition in the UK: They dare not speak its name? *Social Justice, 41*(3), 107–119.

The Prison Reform Trust Bromley Briefing (2021) Winter 2021 Factfile final.pdf. Retrieved 21 July 2022, from prisonreformtrust.org.uk

Tyler, I. (2020). *Stigma: The machinery of inequality.* Bloomsbury Publishing.

Sandberg, S., & Ugelvik, T. (2016). The past, present, and future of narrative criminology: A review and an invitation. Crime, Media, Culture, *12*(2), 129–136.

Ugelvik, T. (2022). The transformative power of trust: Exploring tertiary desistance in reinventive prisons. *The British Journal of Criminology, 62*(3), 623–638.

UserVoice. (2022) Coping with Covid in Prison, The Impact of the Prisoner Lockdown, User-Voice-QUB-Coping-with-Covid.pdf. Retrieved 21 July 2022, from uservoice.org

Watson, R., Stimpson, A., & Hostick, T. (2004). Prison health care: A review of the literature. *International Journal of Nursing Studies, 41*(2), 119–128.

Weaver, A. (2008). *So you think you know me?* Waterside Press.

Weaver, B. (2019). Co-production, governance and practice: The dynamics and effects of User Voice Prison Councils. *Social Policy & Administration*, 53(2), 249–264.

Wong, K., & Horan, R. (2021). Mentoring: Can you get too much of a 'good thing'? Proposing enhancements to the 'effectiveness framework' the England and Wales prison and probation service. *European Journal of Probation*, *13*(3), 207–225.

2   The Legitimacy of Trust

Andi Brierley, Prison Number - CE7976

Who Am I?

As outlined in the opening chapter, I am now in the role of a University Teacher at Leeds Trinity University (LTU). I am part of a wonderful team of academics and practitioners delivering a MSc degree to prison officers on a graduate scheme known as Unlocked Graduates. The idea of recruiting graduate prison officers into the prison regime was a key recommendation of a recent report undertaken to improve education in prisons (Coates, 2016). As an ex-prisoner, I felt that positively contributing to the prison system would be a way of circling back to help other prisoners. However, I have swiftly found that supporting and taking care of prison officers is just as important but came as a surprise as this was a vantage point I had not entirely considered previously. If I get it right, the prisoners benefit as a by-product of supporting prison officers to be the best officers they can be. Essential considering that the role of the prison officer can impact officers' health and well-being if they are not supported (Einat & Suliman, 2021).

My background is in youth justice. I spent 15 years working with children in all aspects of the justice system; from early intervention to managing 'high risk' cases as well as children in secure settings during the first COVID-19 Lockdown. Due to the findings of the independent review of the overrepresentation of children looked after and care leavers in all levels of the justice system (Laming, 2016), my final five years in operation were to safely reduce the number of children in care entering the youth justice system in Leeds. My work was partly strategic, delivering training around Laming's findings and front-line participation work which was recognised as a good practice in the 2019 inspection (see HMIP Leeds, 2019). I have been blessed with the opportunity of working directly with children and young people who have experienced trauma, adversity, and interpersonal challenges. Often in

DOI: 10.4324/9781003349747-2

the absence of consistent, caring, attuned, and predictable relational networks. The science around childhood development suggests that this lack of relational wealth is what develops tolerable stress into toxic stress (Shonkoff et al., 2012). Let's call this relational poverty (Brierley, 2021; Hambrick et al., 2019). The absence of the relational resource of adult attachment which children need throughout development to be healthy and well as they travel through life. It is not a lack of resilience as much as a lack of relational wealth which develops resilience and mitigates adversity (Ludy-Dobson et al., 2010). The effects of an ecological system around the child that does not provide what the American Psychologist Bronfenbrenner theorised as extremely significant to child development (Bronfenbrenner, 1992).

Having this lived experience insight has shaped my practice with justice involved children. Focussing my energy on relational work and project development over the years has prevented me from ever getting disappointed. Not in the same way I have witnessed compassion fatigue or burnout in some of my colleagues which has been categorised as a negative impact of 'exposure to pain, suffering, and trauma' (Sabo, 2011, para 9). I believe that people learn more through relationships and storytelling than they will ever through assessments, intervention plans, and offending behaviour programmes. A stance echoed by McNeill as he explains 'it is through the quality of the relationship formed between the professional and young person [child]…rather than the content of any intervention, that real progress can be made in the prevention of future offending.' (McNeill, 2006, p. 133). Social systems that respond to vulnerable children in our society such as education and youth justice can fuel further stress when justice involved children's neurodiverse needs are not understood or met (see Day, 2021) Neurodiverse meaning neurological and developmental variations in children such as autism or learning disabilities. This is true for most of the children I have worked with over the years in youth justice, not just children in care (see McElvaney, 2016). My relational position is that this is about them, not me or the system. I have always seen my role as a relational collaborator – helping children and young people move on from their offending to develop them, not the systems or even my perspective of their 'script for the future' which scholars have argued is fundamental to the desistance process (Maruna & Roy, 2007, p. 120).

As I will outline shortly, this has never been simply employment for me. The role has *not* given me an opportunity to desist from offending or prevented a return to problematic behaviours such as drug addiction. Maturity, education, and responsibility did that. However, as Maruna pointed out in his Liverpool Desistance Study (LDS), the opportunity supported me to 'make good' and help me develop a positive self-narrative script [a more positive sense of self] to psychologically move on from my offending (Maruna, 2001). It was in fact demonstrating to myself and others that I was more than an ex-offender or ex-prisoner. Helping others had 'adaptive consequences' (LeBel et al., 2015, p. 118). The intervention transmitted me into the tertiary tenet of desistance, and I became a 'wounded healer' (LeBel, 2007). I was able to acquire a degree and even obtain the title of Child Looked After Specialist. Giving others hope beyond my personal prison sentences alleviated the harms of prison as the experience itself is 'painful and damaging' (Liebling, 2011, p. 546). Working and living on both sides of the secure setting has driven me to write this book for two reasons: one is that prison is an extremely complex relational space which needs help from all stakeholders if it is to truly improve recidivism rates; and two, while we experience such a shaming and stigmatising process such as the prison experience, prison officers can provide hope and mitigation. Prison officers can be the change makers – the desistance facilitators.

My Prison Experience

I accept that it is probably quite unusual for someone to present an extensive youth justice career and have repeated personal lived experience of being a prisoner. This section will inevitably amalgamate both my professional and personal experiences of the carceral sphere and criminal justice practice fence. Demonstrating my enduring experience of liminality that I have navigated for the past 15 years. Liminality is explained as the 'betwixt and between middle phase of any ritualised process, during which the individuals involved are understood to be 'no longer' and simultaneously also 'not yet'' (Jewkes & Laws, 2021, p. 395). My lived experience of having some connection to the justice system goes back as far as I can remember.

My mother was an abused 16-year-old child who ran away from a children's home in the care system in 1981 when she fell pregnant with me by a 16-year-old boy (a father I have never seen). Mum proceeded to move around the country, including some time in Scotland in my early years. This was likely so mum could not be found by children's services. Probably because of her own poor experience of care and family separation – coupled with her inability to parent five children by the very young age of 25. Her need for love and companionship was predominately received by unworking men with crime and drugs being a key feature of their lives. As a result, these intersectional experiences become a key feature of my childhood.

These experiences shaped my world view, and most importantly con-structed the perspective of my group membership and relational spaces that made me feel safe and accepted. The justice system often focuses on risk-taking behaviour as this is the behaviour we aim to change, and rightly so. However, from my perspective, a missing part of the nar-rative when we talk about youth crime particularly is acceptance and belonging. The reason I highlight this is because by 17 years old, I was remanded to Brinsford Young Offenders Institution (YOI) which is a Cat B & C prison for Possession with Intent to Supply Class A Drugs. Me and my 15-year-old brother were found in a 23-year-old drug dealers car with vast amount of heroin that was cut and ready to be sold. I had experienced abuse and neglect by various so-called father figures which resulted in me following my mother's footsteps into the care system. Poor role modelling from adults with unmet needs within the family home combined with chronic instability which evidence suggests is profoundly damaging for developing children (see Sandstrom & Huerta, 2013). This chronic level of instability and adversity contributed to my permanent exclusion from school at 15 – often described through the metaphor of school to prison pipeline (Wald & Losen, 2003).

The authorities have now coined the term Child Criminal Exploitation (CCE). The Home Office (2018) have defined CCE as something that 'occurs where an individual or group takes advantage of an imbalance of power to coerce, control, manipulate or deceive a child or young person under the age of 18. The victim may have been criminally exploited even if the activity appears consensual' (p. 3). In 1998 when I was a vulnerable 17-year-old addict, this was not a con-sideration of the Youth Justice Service (YJS). As me and my 15-year-old brother both were heroin-addicted children, when our house was raided by the police there was nothing valuable other than thousands of pounds worth of heroin. However, not a single prison officer, or professional, in that first prison sentence of 18 months ever discussed this interesting power dynamic with me. Not because they weren't interested but because the sole focus was on changing my apparent behaviour or maintaining safety in a violent prison environment. Negating to help me change my behaviour, that missing context of why I behaved in such ways or why I gravitated towards such relation-ships was imperative – but a missed opportunity to develop a positive self-narrative script (see Maruna, 2001).

I completed this 18-month sentence, then received a further 20-month sentence for assault at 19 not long after release while under the influ-ence of alcohol. Being recalled on licence which is characterised as the 'revolving door' (see Padfield & Maruna, 2006). I served further

8 months for Affray aged 21 whilst again under the influence of alcohol. Then at 22, I received a 2-year sentence for Aggravated Burglary and Taking Without Owners Consent (TWOC) a vehicle. Again, whilst under the influence of both alcohol and heroin. In between all these sentences, I was employed in warehouse work, customer service, and construction. As you can see, every single offence I was sent to prison for was related to substance use. My substance use was encouraged by the adults in my childhood and alleviated the biological and physiological responses to toxic stress (see Shonkoff et al., 2012). My childhood of course is like a fingerprint and is unique to me. However, we do know through research that many of those that end up in prison have a similar childhood story (Coates, 2016; Ford et al., 2019).

Our childhoods do not dictate our choices. However, they indeed shape our relational environments, and our choices operate within that complex relational infrastructure. Childhoods do *not* cause offending. However, there is no denying that the choices we make should never be seen as mutually exclusive to our childhood experience, in any context. It is worth remembering when working with people in a justice context that although the behaviour is problematic, it is often a logical response to the individual based on their lived reality. Understanding this individual milieu and responding appropriately and sensitively is the very essence of trauma–informed practice (see Auty et al., 2022; Glendinning et al., 2021; Vaswani & Paul, 2019). It is not repeatedly asking someone to speak about their trauma nor is it delivering interventions that directly tackle prisoner's childhood trauma that makes a prison officer trauma informed or responsive. From my experience of good and bad prison officer practice, it was the officers that could hold space with me in a natural and organic way. Making me believe that in any other circumstance, we could have an authentic connection. Whether they believed that or not, they made me believe it.

It is not so much my lived experience of family dysfunction, poverty, school exclusion, addiction or prison that has provided the enabling conditions to build trusting relational connections with those I have worked with throughout my career. It is just as much my trauma-informed approach and unconditional acceptance that has been in some way shaped by my experience of being with prisoners in a shared carceral space. This is because this perspective often creates an unjudgmental and accepting position of others that have offended. One that is not just about empathy, genuineness, and compassion. One that is about equality and equity in the relational dynamic for an often stigmatised and excluded group. If we define people by their worst moments, we can in fact connect those moments to their identity which is counterproductive for desistance. A strengths–based approach is simply encouraging someone that they can be more than what they have done and making them believe you believe it. Recovering from the prison experience to become a visual beacon of inspiration is the very essence of creating a contagion of hope (Best, 2019). Building someone's belief in themself as a contributing member of society is an approach from my experience that can be far more effective. Mitigating the fact that the pain of imprisonment can be 'brutalising and cause institutionalised harm' (Warr, 2008, p. 21). The role of a prison officer where possible is to cause 'no more harm' and develop that belief in self.

This leads me nicely to present research by various scholars that resonates with both my personal and professional experience being on both sides of the incarceration fence. The scholars articulate how I naturally reflected on the power I held over the incarcerated, and how others held power over me. More importantly, how these powers shape relational practice. Such experiences taught me first-hand how to reach into the depth of reflection as a point of reference to touch base with both sides of this carceral sphere. This duel point of reference increased the likelihood of the incarcerated children legitimising my professional role within the power dynamic of a secured context. This unique lived experience understanding applies to child, young person, or adult. An adversarial space that requires reflection and contextual consideration when attempting to build trust with us as prisoners. If this space is occupied well, we ensure our connections prevent a breaking of the human spirit or the brutalising nature of incarceration; and instead nurture the hope required for desistance (Graham & McNeill, 2017). One study took place in 33 prisons in Ohio, US, and explored prison officer legitimacy, taking a deep dive into power dynamics in prison (Steiner & Wooldredge, 2018). The research explored five different power bases defined in the 80's (see also: Hepburn, 1985; Liebling, 2000) which examined how criminal justice actors exercise their power, reducing negative behaviour in prisons. These power bases can be seen in Figure 2.1.

Positional Power is derived from the structural position the officer takes up in the prisoners' circumstances within the bureaucracy. However, it is highlighted that officers who abuse their positional power are likely to undermine their right to govern. For positional power to be an effective mechanism of maintaining safety and enhancing positive relationships which creates a rehabilitative culture, it must be in part at least dependant on the prisoner's perception of the institution's legitimacy. Therefore, relational skills are required, and being assigned power over someone from the state alone is unlikely to create a rehabilitative culture and construct legitimacy. Officer Y in *Understanding Prison Staff*

Figure 2.1 A visual diagram of the varying power bases described by Steiner & Wooldredge (2018) (see also: Hepburn, 1985 & Liebling, 2000).

demonstrates an example of how to use positional power well (see Warr, 2008).

Referent Power refers to prisoners having mutual respect for the prison officer. Although the research states that referent power is more challenging to obtain due to the coercive nature of incarceration, this is the most likely power base to improve behaviours within prisons from an inside perspective. If a prisoner values and respects a prison officer, they may in fact follow rules more often, even in the absence of the officer. This is because they care about what the officer may think of their behaviour. Having been incarcerated myself and using this experience to shape my practice, this power base was accessible for me to access from *most* young people I worked with in a secure setting or on release. Viewing me as someone they identify with through shared experience. Although difficult to achieve, this should be the aim and focus through an attuned, trauma-informed approach (Auty et al., 2022; Bradley, 2017).

Expert Power is the use of expert skills to obtain relational compliance from prisoners. This could be to help prisoners obtain apps, to write letters to loved ones, to navigate tricky situations with other prisoners or officers; or to persuade prisoners of the benefits of programmes on offer in the prison. Again, a very helpful power base to aim for. Within the study, it was explained that those officers that were more confident of using expert power were more likely to reduce behaviour infractions, whilst also feeling less likely that they would be harmed by prisoners.

Reward Power is when officers feel they have the privilege of incentivising positive behaviour through benefits in exchange for compliance. I felt this power base can be confusing for prisoners because it is often used arbitrarily and creates favouritism. Therefore, it does not surprise me that in their study, Steiner and colleague found that an overuse of reward power is expected to have higher levels of rule breaking or infractions (Steiner & Wooldredge, 2018). If the perceptions of prisoners are that the rules are applied arbitrarily and creates an inequality in treatment, this disrupts legitimacy and creates a sense of injustice. Therefore, reward power if disproportionately used across a prison, is unlikely to reduce rule breaking overall. Liebling (2000) also highlights that the granting of privileges naturally transfers into coercive power as what can be granted, can also be taken away.

Coercive Power is the use of sanction because of noncompliance. Loss of privileges, room restrictions, segregation, and extra duties are several sanctions that can be implemented by officers for not following instructions, or not adhering to prison rules and regulations. However, the researchers expect that an *over reliance* on coercive power is likely to increase rule breaking in prisons. Again, this is caused by prisoners not legitimising the prison officers and the positional power they have over them. The incarceration experience is itself coercive and if this power base is used excessively, it is more likely to create tension and further divide the relationships between the prisoners and officers. Emphasised within the work exploring legitimacy and procedural justice in the Prison Journal, Jackson et al. (2010), highlighted that prison officers must 'increase the experience of procedural fairness among prisoners, and therefore enhance the legitimacy of prison regimes.'

This research by Liebling (2000) and Steiner and Wooldredge (2018) is important because it attempts to ascertain the views of how prisoners legitimise the authority of prison officers. The aim of prison is to hold people to account for crime, and reduce offending upon release, not just control whilst in custody. Therefore, this research and perspective is imperative to the outcome of reducing further victims. I have been locked behind a door and locked people behind theirs. Creating a unique perspective and this research really resonates. I have a personal belief that a good prison officer will likely use all these power bases in different circumstances in appropriate ways. As Crewe (2011) illustrates around the use of 'soft power' and Max Dennehy outlines in chapter four of this book, flexibility and negotiation are imperative skills. This is due to the coercive nature of positional power and the imbalance of the power relationship between prison officers and prisoners. The power is not, should not, and will never be equal. Therefore, a personal relational adjustment is often required to redress that power dynamic and maintain positive behaviour wherever possible. This is the ability to attune to those we work with and ensure they feel as included in decision making as much possible.

As with myself, all officers will tend to use some power bases more than others. However, as the research clearly indicates, prison officers should in fact aim to achieve referent and expert power whenever possible. Utilise their positional power in a way that obtains prisoner legitimacy if we are to create a community culture within prisons that constructs a relational environment. In the end, that is what I believe we are suggesting when we say we need to create a rehabilitative culture within prisons. Rehabilitation may not be the right term. In fact, leading scholars in the criminology field claim that 'the concept of rehabilitation has always been both remarkably elastic and hotly contested' (McNeill, 2012, p. 4). Diving into the term rehabilitation could lead to a macro level discussion. However, this book is concerned with practice and relationships. The rehabilitative culture for this chapter therefore is a culture that increases the likelihood of a prisoner not reoffending upon release and a prison culture that promotes wellbeing. There is also evidence that a focus on obtaining legitimacy within the prison context also promotes wellbeing amongst prison staff because of a focus on justice (see Tankebe & Liebling, 2013).

I have been in several jobs where physical intervention is required from me within my role towards vulnerable young people and children. These incidents can damage the relationships for sure. However, the magic of relational repair takes place through personal reflection and the re-earning of trust and recognising one's positional power. Making an extra effort to ensure that the prisoner believes that it's the procedures of the role and institutional requirements of the prison itself, and not personal. Constantly reminding prisoners that it is *never* personal. Making the prisoners aware that in fact you would have preferred a better outcome can go a long way to creating that relational repair. This could be described as a practical example and a central tenet of Procedural Justice (Jackson et al., 2010). Procedural justice theories suggest that people are more likely to follow rules 'when these authorities treat them in a procedurally just manner' (Beijersbergen et al., 2016, p. 65). Research also indicates that procedural justice increases greater job satisfaction for prison officers which in turn improves the prison experience for all involved (Bierie & Mann, 2017). Taking an approach of human first, prison officer second develops the very essence of humanity and ensures prisoners legitimise the prison itself and the workforce within it. 'We are both here in this space, however, there are rules to follow, and they are not arbitrarily decided by me' which is how I explained these procedures to incarcerated youth while working in secure settings. This is the power of showing up.

Nevertheless, I have personal experience of being worked with by prison officers as a prisoner. It was in fact a prison officer that played the most significant role in my journey to tertiary desistance and beyond. A prison officer that worked in the gym and on positive leisure activities that we as prisoners inappropriately called 'gym screws.' One of these officers gave me the most memorable advice I can recall. After I completed the Community Sports Leadership Award (CSLA) in HMP Leeds, he responded to my negativity about using these qualifications in the community as an ex-prisoner with positivity. He told me that I should stop being negative and realise that most people love a good turnaround story. That if I talked myself up, instead of talking myself down as a prisoner with a useless qualification, the chances of that turnaround would be more likely. That if I chased down my dreams of using these qualifications in the community to work with children, someone out there would likely give me a chance.

This would not be because I was an ex-prisoner with a qualification he explained. It would be because I was me. I was a hard-working person that wanted to give something back to the community from which I had taken. What he made me realise is what *he* saw. He saw more than the clothes I was wearing or the prison number I was provided. He didn't see a *smackhead* or a *prisoner*. The fact that I have won various awards, written two published books, and become a teacher teaching prison officers proved he was right. Crime was my moment, my childhood was my past, but my future looked bright, and his words of wisdom helped me develop my own script for the future. He became a desistance facilitating prison officer, using his positional power and expert power and he probably didn't even know that in these terms. If I was being *honest*, he probably obtained referent power because once he made me feel that way, I didn't want him to see me in a negative light.

In contrast to this, I quite vividly remember another gym screw that demonstrated poor practice in Brinsford YOI when I was just 17. Within my first week in this Category B and C prison, I was withdrawing from heroin, and I didn't make anyone aware due to the internal shame and stigma I felt. Imagine, I was ashamed of myself within a prison cohort. That is how low I was as a child. My body hadn't developed fully yet, and here I was taking on a task that was dehumanising. I would not give it justice attempting to articulate the emotional and physical pain if I tried. Just take a moment to consider that some adults have body parts amputated. How heroin addiction breaks down marriages and keeps parents from taking care of their children and drives so much crime in our society. If you do this, you can at least attempt to empathise with where I was as an incarcerated child. However, the lived reality of this as a child is something else. Going through this withdrawal experience makes humans feel disconnected, isolated, and alone. The prison experience then of course makes people feel unseen and excluded. How we treat individuals upon entry into prison makes such a difference to the individuals we release. If we want to develop empathetic and compassionate humans, we must demonstrate what we wish to see in their worst moments.

This gym screw opened my door because I hesitantly pressed my emergency light late for gym. Simply because I didn't want to get into trouble and had not yet worked out the functions of the prison operation. I was only stood by my door with my towel in my hands and he pushed me back in my cell with force and said, 'too late lad.' This may seem like a small interaction. However, I remember it because it compounded my view at that time that I was a worthless child that didn't mean anything to anyone. All it would have taken is for him to say 'sorry young man, you're too late. Next time, simply get the light pressed early and I will make sure I get to you to the gym.' This would have been received in a profoundly different way because I was exploring how to navigate this carceral space. I would have felt seen by the officer at a critical moment when it mattered most for relationship building and trust. It is obvious that people are very likely to have moments of vulnerability whilst separated from society, family, social norms, and restricted to prison cells. This was a misuse of positional or legitimate power because I didn't comply with a prison rule I didn't yet understand. This just created a sense of distastefulness for officers that didn't lend itself to a rehabilitative culture. Nor was this procedurally just.

A more balanced and interesting interaction with a prison officer was when I was in Doncaster YOI which is a Cat B men's private prison. There had not been a Leeds Wing Rep on wing 3C in Doncaster for several years. Wing Reps attend executive meetings to share the perspectives of prisoners to senior management. This was due to prison officers perceiving Leeds lads as being quite a lively group to manage and the officer's felt bullying was more likely to take place if a Leeds prisoner had more freedom and responsibility on the wing. When a

Sheffield Wing Rep prisoner was released, it left a position that needed filling. Let's call this prison officer, Officer Fred. He was an officer that lots of prisoners struggled with because he was very direct and assertive. I would argue he demonstrated consistency which was an appropriate use of positional power across all of us as prisoners. I would also suggest he was procedurally just with us as prisoners. Until this example. I felt he was always quite consistent, and he would always let you know before he gave any of us a negative write up. Not that I ever heard him say he would give anyone a positive write up, but that was a cultural issue as I never heard any officer say this in my time in prison.

However, Officer Fred was Ex-Military. One sunny morning while handing out letters, he noticed that I received an airmail letter from a friend in Sierra Leone that was in the Armed Forces. Officer Fred decided to give me the Wing Rep job because he said he knew I was from a *good* social group. That my cell was always clean, and I was always presented well. Little did he know this was mainly because my previous prisons at Brinsford YOI and Onley YOI were HMP Prisons and Doncaster was a Category B local private prison. This meant I had to really clean my cell in Brinsford and Onley. We had horrible green blankets which took time and effort to fold and present well as bed packs. Whereas in Doncaster, we had quilts and it was a little less militant. Prisoners were far more laid back and didn't make their beds. Officer Fred gave me the job, which for me was great. However, for consistency reasons, it was an inappropriate use of reward power and procedurally unjust. It derived from his own bias towards me and impacted on his legitimacy. Other prisoners did not understand the decision. This caused issues on the wing, both for me and him. I was new, and others had been on the wing a lot longer than I. They felt they were more deserving and looking back, I agree. My experience is that power makes a difference. The good prison officers know how to use the right power at the right time. This takes presence and reflective practice.

My Advice from the Inside

In my first book I shared my personal story to provide lived experience of recovery to help professionals and others on that journey whilst simultaneously taking ownership of one's behaviour (Brierley, 2019). My second book was to present how I capitalised on my lived experience of criminal justice alongside research and practice to build and sustain trusting connections with young people and children in trouble (Brierley, 2021). How I transferred the techniques I needed when interacting with many different people within the prison system whilst in it; to enhance my ability to develop connections with those involved in crime as a justice professional. A set of guiding principles that are effective when obtaining *trust* from those in the justice system that do not readily offer trust or automatically legitimise authority. Some key elements that are required for justice professionals to gain legitimacy from those of us that enter the prison system. Trust in my view is intrinsically linked to this statement of leading prison academic, Ben Crewe. A concluding statement when exploring staff-prisoner relationships. Asking what *consent,* we have obtained when changing who people are:

> 'prisoners' frustrations about penal power raise important questions about how much we should direct the behaviour of the confined and seek to change their thinking. This is not just an issue of effectiveness, although it is sensible to ask whether governing prisoners so closely might undermine attempts to make them 'responsible.' It is also a matter of what we think are the appropriate limits to personal autonomy, and what right we have (with what consent) to try to change who people are.
>
> (Crewe, 2011, p. 466)

Changing who people are is almost impossible. Although I resonate with Crewe's sentiment here and would suggest that if we obtain trust, we are more likely to obtain consent. A focus on helping people change behaviour however is far more achievable and separates the person from the behaviour which is helpful. However, as we will find throughout the chapters of this book, trust is just the starting point for consent. Max Dennehy, Kevin Neary, Kierra Myles, Devon Ferns, Dan Whyte, and James Docherty will demonstrate how officers have obtained trust which played a role in shaping their behaviour. However, we must have a plan of how to obtain that trust or consent if we are to effectively work alongside people to help *them* change *their* behaviour. We must never assume that we are entitled to the trust of prisoners, simply because one has been granted authority by the state. As we have found, we must seek legitimacy using 'soft power' (Crewe, 2011), one's own discretion and position ourselves in a way that is likely to obtain trust. The following model provides a consistent set of guiding principles which increases the likelihood of developing trusting relationships. It doesn't derive from what works evidence base, but how as a justice professional, my practice was shaped by my lived experience. How I used that insight to create this model as a tool for consistency in my practice.

A coming together of the personal and professional experiences to assist in the trust development process.

I first heard the model presented by Dr Dan Siegal in his YouTube talk 'How Relationships Shape Us' (St Johns Health,, 2017) as Presence, Attunement, Resonance, and Trust (PART). I resonated with this as a way I transferred my lived experience of living with prisoners to obtain trust from people of all ages in contact with the justice or social care systems. My slightly amended Presence, Attunement, Connection and Trust (PACT) model provides an acronym that is very simple to follow. PACT offers practical steps that ensure justice professionals, in this case prison officers have a consistent and effective way of obtaining trusting connections. If prison officers follow these simple steps, it will certainly increase the likelihood of becoming The good prison officer. I will talk you through each step or guiding principle and provide a diagram which can be placed in the office, at home or somewhere that you can access when the job becomes challenging. Those times when the prisoners are not ready to accept your legitimacy or positional power for various reasons. Just remember that is as much about their journey as it is about your own. However, following these principles will likely make your job easier and increase the likelihood of these days becoming less and less. A good prison officer is likely to be flexible, adaptable and know which approach or skill to use at the right time (Arnold, 2016). However, having a set of principles for effective practice is likely to enable officers to ensure they have some level of consistency in a challenging context. These principles can provide that consistency.

Presence

Presence is the power of showing up in the moment. This can be described as a recognition of the complex relational dynamic. Lived Experience as described by my friend and fellow co-author James Docherty as obtaining a 'whole gestalt in one picture' (Brierley, 2021, p. 129). A reflexive recognition of the impact of social exclusion, stigma, and alienation as well as racism for many prisoners. More importantly how that influences the connectedness between prisoners and factors behind delegitimising officers or authority. Taking hold of how that feels when incarcerated and isolated from what humans need to be well such as positive relationships and community, developing further exposure to toxic stress for many prisoners. This deep level of critical reflection can shape how we view and interact with complex challenges within the dynamic of power differentials such as in an incarcerated environment. The need for this critical reflection or presence is imperative because:

> Everyone has 'habits of mind' and 'a point of view' and these two dimensions form a frame of reference that define individuals. The frame of reference can be transformed through critical reflection on these assumptions, habits and beliefs leading to significant personal transformation.
>
> (Paterson & Chapman, 2013)

Reflecting on institutional power differentiation and the frame of reference for all stakeholders in this complex circumstance is not just good practice, it is essential to social and personal growth. Although when working with incarcerated people it doesn't feel like we have power. Especially when being faced with violence or aggressive behaviour. I have been in any number of these incidents as a professional. The power is in the ability to write about someone's behaviour, make decisions about when they leave their cell or even which cell they reside, as well as whether they are allowed family visits. This provides officers an obvious position of power. As many prisoners have negative experiences of school, family breakdown, and even abuse or neglect by people in positions of power in their lives, presence is understanding this relational power dynamic. As trust is not easy to obtain within this context, a lack of reflection or presence often means officers lack the ability to obtain our trust. It was in fact the officers I knew that understood the relational power dynamic that were the most relational and present in the moments I needed it most. This is what sets the relational context for trauma-informed practice (Bradley, 2017). This is the essence of presence and a road to referent power.

Attunement

The antidote to toxic stress is *always* positive relationships. Most of the information coming from the child developmental science fields over the last half a century has highlighted the value of secure attachment. Through Bowlby's Attachment Theory (Bretherton, 1992), or in more recent years the adverse childhood experiences (ACEs) findings (Felitti et al., 1998), we have been repeatedly told that we as humans need positive relationships to mitigate adversity and be well. Attunement then is the positioning of an individual to be a relationship that mitigates or buffers the over-activation of our stress response system. Prisoners are not babies, some may suggest. This is very true. However, although the need for attachment and connections reduces over time, humans never stop seeking a sense of belonging. We are social creatures, and it is in our biological genes that we seek safe relationships. We will avoid uncomfortable relationships and seek relationships that make us feel safe and accepted, even if they are not seemingly productive to outsiders. This is a significant driver behind acquisitive offending and drug addiction, especially in youth. Not something knew. It has long since been established that anti-social peers are a significant driver for offending or criminogenic need (Farrington, 2005). Highlighting those relationships can shape our behaviour negatively, so they can also shape behaviour positively.

The ACEs study demonstrates that not only does adversity change the development of children, but it also evidences that too much adversity can in fact have a lifelong lasting impact. It can negatively affect the medical and social outcomes due to toxic stress and develop a physiological change in the child. Too much adversity in childhood can also increase the likelihood of violence, low academic attainment, teenage pregnancy and yes, even offending, substance misuse, and prison (Ford et al., 2019). Not everyone in the prison system has had an overload of adversity during childhood. Having said that, as we have already highlighted, many have. Anyone that understands prison will also know that being in prison can and often does expose the human body to toxic stress and isolation. Toxic stress and an overly activated stress response system releases cortisol and adrenaline excessively. It is this over release that can cause biological and physiological challenges (Franke, 2014). Especially important to reflect on when leading criminology scholars have found impulsivity is also one of the most significant risk factors associated with crime (Farrington, 2005). However, we as justice professionals can in fact attune to the individuals we are working with so whenever possible, we use our relationships as the vehicle to ensure prisoners are releasing positive hormones which can create the equilibrium for good health. Just like Officer Ted did for Kevin in the next chapter. It is imperative that this be the case for care experience and prisoners with challenging childhoods. However, because of the toxic nature of prison, all prisoners benefit from attuned officers. This is because all prisoners benefit psychologically and physiologically from positive relationships. When we hear 'relationships are everything,' I am not sure if we truly understand that the relationship is the intervention for these individuals.

What does attunement look like in practice? In 2013, just after qualifying in youth justice, I was responsible for case managing a young man on a three-year Youth Rehabilitation Order (YRO). The index offences were prolific sexual offences towards females. I needed to reflect on so many levels because this was my first experience of working with sexual offending. Regardless of my own involvement in offending, I knew my lived experiences did not set me up to have authentic connections with individuals that committed this type of offence. In fact, in my time in prison, I would actively avoid and sometimes shame people that had committed sex offences to fit into my social situation and make sure I was accepted. This is what Max describes as the hypervigilant 'front stage' in Chapter 4. Upon reflecting on how this interfered with my ability to attune as a professional, I made a practical decision to see this young man every Friday evening at 4 pm before I finished work. I told him this was because 'he was better behaved than the rest of the young people I work with (which was true), and it was great to end my working week with him.'

I coordinated a multi-agency team around him over the three years, involving his alternative provision (education), therapeutic support, children's mental health (CAHMS), and police. He never reoffended in the three years I supervised him or the following nine years to this day. I know this because I gained consent from his mother to use this example as a case study. Although no details have been shared, this should always be sought for courtesy and ethical reasons. Again, emphasising the transformational outcome to personal reflection and attuning to the individuals' relational needs as a justice professional. There are probably several reasons why he desisted, and I may not know all of them. However, I truly believe that my attunement and personal adjustment made a relational difference to how he felt about being supervised by an adult for sex offences. Not too dissimilar to the stigmatising feeling of being seen by professionals and the public as a prisoner; a criminal or con. He needed to feel attuned to because the driver for his offending stemmed from his social isolation because of his educational needs and accessing sexualised pornographic material which he didn't understand due to his maturity and capacity. My job was to make him feel normal, happy, and accepted which became the intervention. Principles that underpin the Good Lives Model (see Ward and Gannon, 2006). This is the essence of personal attunement. It is the doing part that comes after presence to assist the individual to develop their own narrative script, not to come up with this for them.

Connection

Since joining youth justice as a professional in 2007 when children entered the YJS in mass which is termed net-widening (Case & Haines,

2021), I have always struggled with the term 'engagement.' When the term is used in a justice context, it is often from a vantage point of varying power bases. Implying someone doesn't engage with a direction or programme is inevitably a mix of positional, reward and coercive power. 'Engage with the direction and you will benefit; do not and there could be consequences.' There is no getting away from the very fact that this positional power exists within the relational dynamic in prison or the justice system. Acknowledging this as we have found is presence and responding appropriately is attunement. A way to obtain legitimacy within this context is to personally adjust the word engagement to connection. This slight change in language addresses the power dynamic as it ensures the professional or practitioner is also responsible for that *connection*. Without this shared responsibility or reciprocity, prison officers are simply taking the stance that their positional power gives them authority to direct prisoners. As we have already found within this chapter, legitimacy and trust are vital components. This entails that wherever possible, good practice would be to change the word engagement to connection. This way we can create a goal to our own relational approach that is not lazy and coercive. The process then becomes reciprocal and creates a restorative relationship which is grounded in the principles of relational equality.

Using connection is not going to address the coercive nature of incarceration, or make prisoners feel they are not in prison. Nor will using connection empower the prisoner and leave you as a prison officer vulnerable. We do not have to ask a prisoner, are we connecting. Although for many prisoners that would probably take them by surprise and demonstrate humanity in dark and challenging times. I have never felt uncomfortable opening myself up to those I work with in any context. I often use this as a strategy to demonstrate the similarities we have when many in the justice system often focus on the differences to staff. The switch of the word can simply remind us as justice practitioners to understand that prison is tough, and prisoners are navigating many complex geographical spaces with prisoners and prison officers. Notwithstanding the issues prisoners often have with family members and children on the other side of the prison fence. Then on top of the isolating nature of prison, we often must comply with rules and regulations that are very rigorous, but sometimes arbitrary and inconsistent. This can be really taxing at times and if prison officers only uses the term engagement, it takes away the lived reality of prison that may drive that lack of engagement. Which could in fact be our own practice approach at times. 'As I am required to use my authority to guide this person facing all these challenges to do as directed, have I done enough to connect with them to gain the required level of legitimacy.' This is an effective way of recognising the reciprocal nature of all relationships. This is nature of connection and the essence of expert power.

Trust

What right, or in Ben Crewe's(2011) terms consent do we have to change people and their behaviour? Being in prison is one thing. However, the experience also sits within a context of having professionals constantly assessing whether you are rehabilitated in *their* judgement. How does this feel and does this transactional relational experience impact on the trust officers get from prisoners? Are prison officers trained on the inside perspectives of prisoners that are presented within these chapters as much as the prison bureaucracy, risk management and security. Some scholars claim that 'prison is part of a penal apparatus that seeks to reproduce itself' (Johns, 2017, p. 3). Meaning that being in prison is a risk factor to further offending. This would go some way to explain the high reoffending rates highlighted in the previous chapter. The question is whether within this context of prison and punishment, can we truly develop a rehabilitative culture? As you will see, the answer to this question according to the chapters in this book, seems to be, yes. Can we influence the behaviour or thinking of prisoners whilst they are in prison? Again, the chapters in this book demonstrate the answer is, yes. However, the change required seems to be a sense of collaboration between prisoners and prison staff. The solution according to these chapters lies not only within programmes or assessments; they are also found within relationships, attachments, and of course trust. Ugelvik (2022) argues that trust is a catalyst for the desistance process. The chapters of this book certainly argue that without trust, any level of change is incredibly unlikely.

In the end, it must be a matter of trust. Liebling and Arnold (2004, p. 248) defines trust in relation to another person as 'reliance on the honesty, reliability and good sense of a person, the level of responsibility or confidence invested in and experienced by individuals.' We can incarcerate people, vulnerable or not and maintain safety in prisons with the use of force and isolation through a discourse of public protection. However, if we want the prison system to support individuals to leave prison as better community members than the point of incarceration, it must start with trust. Why would any human, let alone a human that has been exposed to victimisation, inequality and poverty which are factors experienced by many of those we incarcerate allow people they do not trust to change them or their behaviour. No matter how well

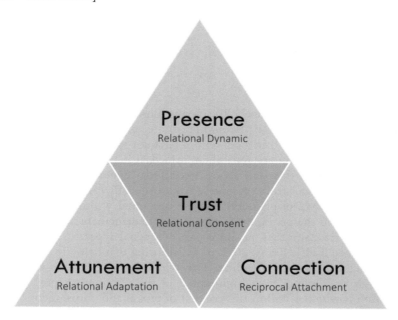

Figure 2.2 Visual diagram to explain the key principles of the Presence, Attunement, Connection and Trust (PACT) Model (see Brierley, 2021; St Johns Health, 2017).

resourced a programme, or how much evidence backs up an intervention plan, we are not likely to achieve change without trust. If we are present enough to understand the relational dynamic; ready and willing to make a relational adjustment to attune with prisoners; try to connect with prisoners in a reciprocal manner the way all humans deserve; we can certainly make a positive difference to people's behaviour, their identity and most of all, the communities they are released into. This is the spirit, and most importantly the value of trust when working with prisoners. This diagram in Figure 2.2 is a visual of the model.

References

Arnold, H. (2016). The prison officer. In Handbook on prisons (pp. 265–283). Routledge.

Auty, K. M., Liebling, A., Schliehe, A., & Crewe, B. (2022). What is trauma-informed practice? Towards operationalisation of the concept in two prisons for women. Criminology & Criminal Justice, https://doi.org/10.1177/17488958221094980

Beijersbergen, K. A., Dirkzwager, A. J. E., & Nieuwbeerta, P. (2016). Reoffending After Release: Does Procedural Justice During Imprisonment Matter? Criminal Justice and Behavior, 43(1), 63–82. https://doi.org/10.1177/0093854815609643

Best, D. (2019). *Pathways to recovery and desistance* (p. 232). Policy Press.

Bierie, D. M., & Mann, R. E. (2017). The history and future of prison psychology. *Psychology, Public Policy, and Law, 23*(4), 478.

Bradley, A. (2017). *Trauma-informed practice: Exploring the role of adverse life experiences on the behaviour of offenders and the effectiveness of associated criminal justice strategies.* University of Northumbria at Newcastle.

Bretherton, I. (1992). The origins of attachment theory: John Bowlby and Mary Ainsworth. *Developmental Psychology, 28*(5), 759.

Brierley, A. (2019). *Your honour can I tell you my story.* Waterside Press.

Brierley, A. (2021). *Connecting with young people in trouble: Risk, relationships and lived experience.* Waterside Press.

Bronfenbrenner, U. (1992). *Ecological systems theory.* Jessica Kingsley Publishers.

Case, S., & Haines, K. (2021). Abolishing youth justice systems: Children first, offenders nowhere. *Youth Justice, 21*(1), 3–17.

Coates, S. (2016). Unlocking potential: A review of education in prison, Ministry of Justice, Dame Sally Coates, May 2016.

Crewe, B. (2011). Soft power in prison: Implications for staff–prisoner relationships, liberty, and legitimacy. *European Journal of Criminology, 8*(6), 455–468.

Day A. M., (2022). Disabling and Criminalising Systems? Understanding the Experiences and Challenges Facing Justice Experienced, Neurodiverse Children in the Education and Youth Justice Systems. Retrieved from SSRN: https://ssrn.com/abstract=3951732 or http://dx.doi.org/10.2139/ssrn.3951732

Einat, T., & Suliman, N. (2021). Prison changed me—and I just work there: Personality changes among prison officers. *The Prison Journal, 101*(2), 166–186.

Farrington, D. P. (2005). Childhood origins of antisocial behavior. *Clinical Psychology & Psychotherapy: An International Journal of Theory & Practice, 12*(3), 177–190.

Felitti, V. J., Anda, R. F., Nordenberg, D., Williamson, D. F., Spitz, A. M., Edwards, V., & Marks, J. S. (1998). Relationship of childhood abuse and household dysfunction to many of the leading causes of death in adults: The adverse childhood experiences (ACE) study. *American Journal of Preventive Medicine, 14*(4), 245–258.

Ford, K., Barton, E., Newbury, A., Hughes, K., Bezeczky, Z., Roderick, J., & Bellis, M. (2019). Understanding the prevalence of adverse childhood experiences (ACEs) in a male offender population in Wales: The Prisoner ACE Survey. Public Health Wales; Bangor University.

Franke, H. A. (2014). Toxic stress: Effects, prevention and treatment. *Children, 1*(3), 390–402.

Glendinning, F., Rodriguez, G. R., Newbury, A., & Wilmot, R. (2021). Adverse-childhood-experience-ACE-and-trauma-informed-approaches-in-youth-justice-services-in-Wales-An-evaluation-of-the-implementation-of-the-enhanced-case-management-ECM-project-The-views-and-experie.pdf (researchgate.net). Retrieved 12 November 2022

Graham, H., & McNeill, F. (2017). Desistance: Envisioning futures. In *Alternative criminologies* (pp. 433–451). Routledge.

Hambrick, E. P., Brawner, T. W., Perry, B. D., Brandt, K., Hofmeister, C., & Collins, J. O. (2019). Beyond the ACE score: Examining relationships between timing of developmental adversity, relational health and developmental outcomes in children. *Archives of Psychiatric Nursing, 33*(3), 238–247.

Hepburn, J. R. (1985). The exercise of power in coercive organizations: A study of prison guards. *Criminology, 23*(1), 145–164.

Her Majesties Inspectorate of Probation Leeds. (2019). An inspection of youth offending service in Leeds. Retrieved 8 April 2022, from justiceinspectorates.gov.uk

Home Office. (2018). Criminal exploitation of children and vulnerable adults: County lines guidance, retrieved 2 July 2022, online from Criminal Exploitation of children and vulnerable adults: County Lines guidance (publishing.service.gov.uk)

Jackson, J., Tyler, T. R., Bradford, B., Taylor, D., & Shiner, M. (2010). Legitimacy and procedural justice in prisons. *Prison Service Journal, 191*, 4–10.

Jewkes, Y., & Laws, B. (2021). Liminality revisited: Mapping the emotional adaptations of women in carceral space. *Punishment & Society, 23*(3), 394–412.

Johns, D. F. (2017). *Being and becoming an ex-prisoner.* Routledge.

Laming, H. (2016). *In care, out of trouble: How the life chances of children in care can be transformed by protecting them from unnecessary involvement in the criminal justice system.* Prison Reform Trust.

LeBel, T. P. (2007). An examination of the impact of formerly incarcerated persons helping others. *Journal of Offender Rehabilitation, 46*(1–2), 1–24.

LeBel, T. P., Richie, M., & Maruna, S. (2015). Helping others as a response to reconcile a criminal past: The role of the wounded healer in prisoner reentry programs. *Criminal Justice and Behavior, 42*(1), 108–120.

Liebling, A. (2000). Prison officers, policing and the use of discretion. *Theoretical Criminology, 4*(3), 333–357.

Liebling, A. (2011). Moral performance, inhuman and degrading treatment and prison pain. *Punishment & Society, 13*(5), 530–550.

Liebling, A., & Arnold, H. (2004a). *prisons and their moral performance: A study of values, quality and prison life.* Oxford University Press.

Ludy-Dobson, C. R., & Perry, B. D. (2010). The role of healthy relational interactions in buffering the impact of childhood trauma. *Working With Children to Heal Interpersonal Trauma: The Power of Play, 26*, 43.

Maruna, S. (2001). *Making good* (p. 86). American Psychological Association.

Maruna, S., & Roy, K. (2007). Amputation or reconstruction? Notes on the concept of 'knifing off' and desistance from crime. *Journal of Contemporary Criminal Justice, 23*(1), 104–124.

McElvaney, R., & Tatlow-Golden, M. (2016). A traumatised and traumatising system: Professionals' experiences in meeting the mental health needs of young people in the care and youth justice systems in Ireland. *Children and Youth Services Review, 65*, 62–69.

McNeill, F. (2006). A desistance paradigm for offender management. *Criminology and Criminal Justice, 6*(1), 39–62.

McNeill, F. (2012). Four forms of 'offender' rehabilitation: Towards an interdisciplinary perspective. *Legal and Criminological Psychology*, *17*(1), 18–36.

Padfield, N., & Maruna, S. (2006). The revolving door at the prison gate: Exploring the dramatic increase in recalls to prison. *Criminology & Criminal Justice*, *6*(3), 329–352.

Paterson, C., & Chapman, J. (2013). Enhancing skills of critical reflection to evidence learning in professional practice. *Physical Therapy in Sport*, *14*(3), 133–138.

Sabo, B., (Jan 31, 2011). Reflecting on the concept of compassion fatigue. OJIN: The Online Journal of Issues in Nursing, 16(1), 1.

Sandstrom, H., & Huerta, S. (2013). The negative effects of instability on child development: A research synthesis.

Shonkoff, J. P., Garner, A. S., Siegel, B. S., Dobbins, M. I., Earls, M. F., & McGuinn, L. (2012). The lifelong effects of early childhood adversity and toxic stress. *Pediatrics*, *129*(1), e232–e246.

St Johns Health (2017)–, How our relationships shape us by Dr. Dan Siegal, [video], Retrieved 23 August 2022, from Youtube [(5) How our Relationships Shape Us by Dr. Dan Siegel]

Steiner, B., & Wooldredge, J. (2018). Prison officer legitimacy, their exercise of power, and inmate rule breaking. *Criminology*, *56*(4), 750–779.

Tankebe, J., & Liebling, A. (2013). Legitimacy and criminal justice: An introduction. *Legitimacy and criminal justice: An international exploration*. Oxford University Press.

Ugelvik, T. (2022). The transformative power of trust: Exploring tertiary desistance in reinventive prisons. *The British Journal of Criminology*, *62*(3), 623–638.

Vaswani, N., & Paul, S. (2019). 'It's knowing the right things to say and Do': Challenges and opportunities for trauma-informed practice in the prison context. *The Howard Journal of Crime and Justice*, *58*(4), 513–534.

Wald, J., & Losen, D. J. (2003). Defining and redirecting a school-to-prison pipeline. *New Directions for Youth Development*, *2003*(99), 9–15.

Ward, T., & Gannon, T. A. (2006). Rehabilitation, etiology, and self-regulation: The comprehensive good lives model of treatment for sexual offenders. *Aggression and Violent Behavior*, 11(1), 77–94.

Warr, J. (2008). Personal reflections on prison staff. *Understanding Prison Staff*, 17–29.

3 More Than a Number!

Kevin Neary, Prison Number - 071087

Who Am I?

I'm Kevin Neary. Some may say I am a tall handsome Scotsman. However, I am a little more modest, so let's just say handsome. I am the co-founder of the charity Aid&Abet in Scotland. A peer-led organisation with people who have had past lived experience in the criminal justice system and are in a healing process from addiction and trauma (Maté, 2012). The aim is to support people leaving prison and integrating back into the community by providing a gate pick-up service on the day of liberation, supporting the individual through the first 72 hours. A crucial time, especially at weekends when an individual is liberated on a Friday with most services closed over the weekend, leaving the person stranded. Aid&Abet Mentor/Recovery Practitioners are mostly volunteers who use their childhood experiences and most present experiences of change to build a relationship of trust, guiding people on a pathway into services that best meet their needs through a peer mentor process (Buck, 2018). Aid&Abet cover three important services within the first 72 hours. Housing, benefits support, and access to a GP. This, therefore, covers shelter, food, and medical care, especially if they are on an Opiate Replacement Therapy (ORT) prescription such as methadone, ibrupamorphine (suboxone), and other medical ailments.

The right support within this 72-hour window reduces the stress that is endured during the reintegration process and prevents a return to offending behaviour as well as a relapse to substances and possible drug overdose. When people are released from prison, their needs must be met immediately to prevent reoffending or relapse back into previous habits such as addiction. The first few days of release are critical to prevent a return to prison due to a breach of licence that recalls people back to prison if they do not comply with stringent licence conditions. Preventing premature death by unintentional drug overdose

DOI: 10.4324/9781003349747-3

and suicide in this first 72-hour period due to reduced tolerance levels is critical. Research indicates that mortality rates are highest within the first two weeks of release (see Binswanger et al., 2012; Farrell & Marsden, 2008). This is particularly true of those with short sentences which often tend to be those with drug, alcohol, and accommodation issues (Hudson et al., 2012).

Aid&Abet have been a registered charity since March 2016, even though volunteers were providing support for 18 months prior to us becoming a charity. Volunteer mentors would travel to any prison in the UK for residents that may be returning to Edinburgh and the Lothians in Scotland. All our volunteers had experienced care homes as children and spent time in prison as adults, which Andi highlighted in the introduction is like many in the prison system. Most if not, all had experienced mental health issues and substance dependency through their teenage and adult years before turning their lives around. Using this experience as a major tool in supporting others who wished to go on that recovery journey. We often hear about intergenerational trauma. We at Aid&Abet focus on intergenerational healing.

Our volunteers simply want to give those leaving prison structure to their day. Give something back to people and society to create a better sense of self to feel good about who they are and what they do. Many of our volunteers felt that due to their past lived experience of prison and childhood challenges, they would find it harder to get a job compared to others. We know that employment reduces the likelihood of reoffending, so we must seek to change this and Aid&Abet embeds this notion into practice (McEvoy, 2008). Everyone who came to volunteer for us were currently unemployed. Little did Aid&Abet know that we not only supported people leaving prison but also simultaneously developed the mentors. So much so that the past 36 volunteers are all now in fulltime employment with other organisations in social care settings. This creates healed individuals and healed individuals better integrated into the community.

Five are seconded to Action for Children supporting young people on the cusp of crime, substance use and a Police Scotland Project (Vow Project) where mentors work side by side with four plain-clothed police officers on early intervention and prevention. They work predominantly with 16/25-year-olds. Attending Edinburgh sheriff court cells and custody suites as well as responding to referrals from social work or family members. The project is voluntary and helps divert children away from criminal behaviour and substance use and into training and employment opportunities. I have been working on this project for the past six years. This is the only project of its kind in the UK that has cops and con working closely together. We have reduced offending by 86% in the young people we have served over the years and saved the Scottish government an estimated £8,500, 000 according to calculations by Haymarket Police Station in Edinburgh.

I'm sure as you read on you are keen to know why all this came about and what my driver was for making this change for our most vulnerable children in Scotland. I feel it's important to start by simply explaining my unique story as, like Andi and the other authors of this book, it was quite unorthodox. I'm sure my story will resonate with many of the people you will meet in the establishments as prison officers and other professionals. My own journey to this point can provide some insight into the offending behaviours, substance use and mental health challenges of those vulnerable and at times challenges prisoners that prison officers care for. Hopefully, this will remind officers that when you are tired, exhausted, and challenged, even those most challenging are in fact, more than a number!

My Prison Experience

I spent 30 long years in the prison system in and out of a turbulent ocean of addiction over those hard decades. In my extensive experience of various sectors, I have met good schoolteachers and bad teachers. Good social workers and bad social workers. Good cops, bad cops. Good prison staff, and bad prison staff. Even good doctors, and bad doctors. I'm sure you get where I'm going with this. There are of course good and bad in every environment, institution, and sector. So, what does it take to make a Good Prison Officer? It is important when asking this question to continuously ask prisoners their perspectives. We are all different, but the experience is familiar, and our perspective is essential to this question.

Growing up I experienced poverty. At times with no electricity or gas as it had been cut off due to my parents being unable to pay the bills. There were 11 of us in total as a family and my parents found it very hard to make ends meet. Being from a large family with financial difficulties was a risk factor for delinquent offending in the longitudinal Cambridge Study looking at factors that develop into criminogenic needs in youth (Farrington, 2005). They were both under so much stress bringing up a family in these circumstances in the 70s and 80s. Their way of dealing with this stress was to drink heavily at weekends. This would end up exposing me to domestic abuse and violence. They didn't know what I know today, unfortunately. The social, economic, and psychological factors would play out in a way that I would end up in the criminal justice system and experience chronic addiction. This was due to unintentional neglect. I don't blame my parents for this because my insight now has taught me that they were as much a victim of circumstance as I was due to the socio-economic factors mentioned above (see Brierley, 2019; Weaver, 2008).

They come under the term used today as adverse childhood experiences (ACEs), or in other terms childhood trauma (Felitti et al., 1998). My parents, teachers, and everyone I crossed paths with as a child were limited in their knowledge of knowing how to respond to thethe consequences this had on my behaviour. Just as suggested by Bruce Peery and Opera Winfrey in their book, the question or professional curiosity should not have been to ask what was wrong with me, but instead explore 'what happened to me' (Winfrey & Perry, 2021).

Of course, due to capacity issues and maturity, I didn't know that it could have been explored and possibly even explained through a holistic human lens of biopsychosocial factors. A model that explains a lot about such childhood experiences and that these contributing factors in my childhood interacted in a damaging way. My first ever traumatic memory was when I was around 4 years old. Seeing a knife fight with my dad and two other men, I didn't realise this would influence my brain development or impair me socially and neurologically. This became a familiar story. How could a child so young understand that the exposure to so many other negative events that were observed through my own personal lens within my own interpretation of the world manifested into trauma and adversity that were damaging my ability to function (see Fry et al., 2018). I was unable to reach socially expected milestones and the more violence I witnessed as a child, the angrier I became, and this developed into an isolated and stressed child.

This really revealed itself during my school years as I didn't manage to take in information from my teachers and struggled to read and write. This must have been as frustrating for my teachers as much as it was for me. The only conclusion that the teachers could come up with was that I was unwilling to learn like the other kids who were doing well, or at least better than I. Due to the stress of going home to domestic violence and poverty conditions, I would act out in class when feeling stressed by disrupting the classroom. In one sense I was looking for attention as well as a distraction. Maybe someone would recognise the pain. I was seemingly speaking through my behaviour but not getting the response I was craving. By the age of 13, I had my first taste of alcohol. I remember that experience like it was yesterday. The noise dampened down in my head like diving into a swimming pool and the noise dims down under the water. The air was like menthol. I could breathe and all the internal fear and anxiety had left me in an instant. I was bursting with a knew found confidence, or so I thought.

This was to be the start of me getting literally Out My Nut! Out my head, out of my conscious thinking. Not realising I was starting to lose 'ME' in this process. I was kicked out of school at 14 with little education and of course no qualifications. I progressed into a young offender's institution by the age of 17. Smoking weed and taking prescription drugs, illicitly along with alcohol which became intrinsically linked to my behaviour and identity. Any prescription drug that stated on the box that it may cause drowsiness and to not drive or operate machinery, I would eat them!

This led to aggressive behaviour. I couldn't hold down a job. Couldn't hold down a relationship for any length of time. I was in and out of work as much as I was in and out of relationships. Moving around homeless from one spot to the other and living in hostels. It was a constant life of doing trips to police stations, courts, and prisons over the years. As already stated, I met good cops, bad cops. Good prison staff and bad prison staff. The bad ones I often referred to as DOGs!! My relationship with any type of authority was never healthy. They had their views about me, and I had my mind set about them. The them versus us attitude which did no one any good!

As the years went on my behaviour escalated from smoking weed to smoking crack and using heroin intravenously. In 2006, the house I was shacked up in was surrounded by armed police officers who came gun ready for an armed robbery I had committed. My mental health was in such a bad way and my thinking was severally distorted. A way of describing my unhealthy thinking at the time is that I thought 'I should just get the cops to shoot me.' Through police negotiators they managed to change my way of thinking. I came out of the house and walked into a five years three-month prison sentence with a three-year extension to monitor me when I would be released as I was unpredictable and dangerous.

In prison so much had changed from the first time I was incarcerated. I went from a cell that had a bed jaggy blanket and a piss pot, to a cell that had a bed with a quilt cover, a toilet, a TV, wash hand basin and an intercom. I could press a button and speak to staff. Room service at its best I thought. Indicating how little time I had spent accessing room service. I was on 120 ml of methadone. I hated the staff. That was the perception, and I would argue in many cases; I was judged as a junkie. I'm not on a work party. I don't feel treated the same as other inmates and I can see others like me are treated the same. I remember asking a staff member about a possible work party. His response was, 'did I offer you the position? NO! Well, go and fuck off.' I wanted to leap over the counter and bite his Adams apple out of his neck. I was shaking with rage as I was verbally abused by a few and saw every other staff member stand by and say nothing.

My way of dealing with them was to make sure they said my name twice by never answering them when the shouted NEARY! I always had my back to the door in my cell when they opened it. This was the only control I had left. 'NEARY,' 'NEARY!' Then I would turn around. I would not speak or even look at staff most of the time. They were all DOGs through my lens and this negative conditioned belief had become my default position. This went on for months. It did not for a moment as you can imagine get me any friends amongst the officers. My life to this point had not given me the skills to deal with this situation. Therefore, I didn't know how to change it. Then one day everything changed with an intervention from a prison officer.

I hear the footsteps, the jingle of the keys. I turn my back to the door as the keys start to unlock. The Door opens and a voice says, 'Kevin can I come in?' I'm thinking this is not a prison officer its usually 'NEARY!' Then the voice says again 'Kevin can I come in?' I look around and it's an officer who introduces himself as Mark. I'm a bit bewildered and slightly confused. This is not the norm. I said he could come in, so he sits on my bed and starts chatting to me about a course in the prison. He asks if I would be interested in attending. I explain that I don't get on a work party. The inmates are all away to their work parties and courses early in the morning. That I can't go on the movement in the morning. I need to wait on my methadone being given out at 10.00 am and they have all gone by then.

Mark simply told me he would get that changed for me to make it possible to attend the course. Mark goes on to tell me more about the course and he does get my meds time changed so much that they made it a policy for every inmate to receive their meds before movement in the mornings. I attended the course after spending nine months locked up in the hall because one prison officer took the time with his kindness and compassion to see me as a person rather than my behaviour and my number '071087 NEARY!' I felt like Kevin, the name my mother gave me. We started building a trusting relationship as each day I attended this course that was Trauma Focussed Cognitive Behaviour Therapy (TFCBT). An evidenced based therapy that helped me connect my thoughts and feelings to my behaviour (Campbell et al., 2016). For the first time in my life, I had an effective intervention from a prison staff. The TFCBT enabled me to discover that I needed to reconnect with myself. That I had lost that internal connection along the way.

Suddenly, I absolutely get it. How I think and view the world causes an emotional feeling in me and out of that develops my actions. Most of my life I thought negative, felt negative, and acted negative. Such a simple concept that can trap you in your own mind.

As I navigated and engaged in the course, I started learning to play the guitar. Then Billy Brag came to visit the prison as he is founder of 'Jail Guitar Doors.' This is in memory of Joe Strummer of the clash. Billy would get many celebs to sign the guitar and Billy would raffle it at concerts to raise money to buy guitars for people in prison. It was then that Billy said I could express my thoughts and feelings through writing poems and turn them into songs. That I can say whatever I wanted in my writing, and no one could tell me 'I can't say that.' I hit the ground running writing poems and songs about the war in Afghanistan, domestic abuse, behaviour, and addiction. I decided to write about what heroin said to me in its own words and it goes like this:

> Hi there, I'm pleased to meet you
> I'm not very big but I'm going to treat you
> Just open me up and lay me on foil I promise you this
> you won't ever toile
> As you come to get me, I will treat you my pleasure,
> As you get to know me you will want me forever
> The vapour I release into your lungs
> Will make you feel so comfortably numb
>
> You've noticed how your cash vanished fast
> Now you want our friendship to be a thing of the past
> I'm in control in so many ways
> From when you open your eyes until the end of the day
> I'll control the way you walk and talk
> I'm Brown powder I'm top of the block
>
> You try to ignore me and give me up
> But I'm in control now I'll fuck you up
> You will shake shiver shite and sweat you will fight, like
> a fish caught up in a net
> You will lie and cry and want me to stop
> You will think I'm turning your legs into rocks
>
> Your insides a churning, your heart is burning
> You're now realising that it's me that your wanting

So, you have me in your life for ever
You will always be chasing that first dose of pleasure
When you have lost all your family and friends
It's me and you until the very END!

I was so invested in the CBT stuff I said to Mark, 'I should be taking this stuff into schools. Thoughts, feelings, behaviours, consequences, and choices. I want to take this into schools when I get out.' Mark responded with, 'what makes you think taking your story and the CBT concept into schools would work.' I tell Mark the snowball story. That when I was in my second year, my school was raising money for the blind. A blind person with his guide dog attended an assembly to receive the money. We were allowed to ask the blind man some questions. One pupil asked, 'Do you dream?' The blind man explained that people born blind don't get visuals, but get other senses in their dreams such as smell and shadows etc. He goes on to say that he gets visuals as he could see until he was 12 years old.

Another pupil asked, 'How did you go blind?' He tells the assembly that he got hit on the head with a snowball that had a rock in it. That it knocked him unconscious, and he never saw again! I looked at Mark and said, 'that is the moment I stopped flinging snowballs.' To this day when I see snowballs, I think of that blind man. It had a profound effect on me. If I could go into schools and tell my story, it's not just snowballs we are talking about. Its premature death, prison, addiction, violence, and fractured families. Maybe I could make good and use my story to help children reflect on how their childhoods affect their feelings and how those feeling affects their thinking which in turn affects their actions.

Mark looked at me and said, 'Kev you're never getting to work in schools, you're an armed robber, a drug addict and on a very high dose of methadone. Maybe you should focus on you getting right first. However, let's face it, you're never working in schools.' I went to my cell and thought about my past and how all of it could have been prevented. Thinking about the kids today who are going to end up on the same journey as me. I cried that night. Not because of what Mark said or about my past. I cried as for the first time in my life I knew I had found a purpose. A reason to be good. A reason to make good and this filled me with emotions that I couldn't hold back.

As I continued with the CBT course, I got more involved with other groups within the prison. I truly felt I was rehabilitating. I went from 120 ml of methadone to my last dose on 24 March 2008. That by the way was my 40th birthday and a day that I will never forget (I know it's my birthday, but now it's extra special). It was the last day I ever had methadone. My family on the outside felt they were getting their son and brother back. My 12-year-old son was getting his father back. I was becoming connected with myself after the trauma of my childhood and my own behaviour had disconnected me to my own soul.

As my journey within prison was taking a more positive road, building better relationships with prison officers and other staff, it reinforced that there are good and bad in every job. I just happened to find the good guys through good communication and better understood that being treated badly by one officer no longer meant there was a them and us. Through no judgment and a desire to help other people, I started to see this in prison staff. Yes, I must admit that amongst the workforce there were still dogs. However, now my focus was never on them. I simply decided to communicate with the Marks of the workforce. I was transferred to an open estate where I picked up more survival tools for when I was due parole. Not knowing what was to come. As prison became a safe place, a place where there was less stress. I had the ability to learn new things, educate myself and heal through writing songs and poems. I self-taught the guitar and became fit and healthy. We could say it was a brand new me.

I got paroled and within 72 hours I had a needle back in my arm. The relationships I built back up within the family started to break down. I was in isolation, and I had two non-fatal, or intentional overdoses. Here is what happened. I leave prison with all the tools Mark and others gave me. What was missing was someone to be there and help me sharpen the tools by helping me integrate back into society, preventing a kind of cliff edge post sentence. The stress came on so fast with housing issues, benefits, and a sense of loss as in prison as I had a community. I had connections. I lost all that and not realising how super sensitive I am, I took away the emotional pain the same way I did on my first drink at 13 years old. A recurring issue one might say. However, the courses I did helped me understand I was stronger now. I had learnt that there are better things to subdue the emotional pain.

I went to rehab voluntarily to tackle this head on. I came out of rehab and maintained the mindset I discovered in prison and founded the charity Aid&Abet. I then got seconded to the police Scotland project where one of my police colleagues was one of the officers who was involved with the armed response team outside my house. From there I got involved in another project called Turn Your Life Around, taking my story into schools! During my child protection training I went outside for a smoke break and there is Mark. I hadn't seen him since prison. He had since left as a prison officer and asked what I was doing now.

I said, 'Mark I'm working in schools, prisons, courts and helping others to avoid the journey I went on. You played a role in this journey, never forget that. Also, always encourage anyone's dream because I am living proof that it is all possible.'

My Advice from the Inside

Every human being has a kindness and compassionate side to them. Mark showed that to me the day he asked me if he could come into my cell. If I was to give a message to people who want to be good prison officers, I would strongly ask yourself the question *why*? If your there for the salary, the security of employment or want to control prisoners, then I don't believe you would make a good prison officer. These are features or characteristics that belong elsewhere, not in prison.

If you have a vested interest in people and want to help rehabilitate prisoners, showing positive communication skills and an interest in people's health and wellbeing, then you will be a top-class prison officer. If you will look forward to going to work as people are interesting characters from all walks of life, who also have a story to tell, this is likely to be a job for you. There are people who will be locked up for the rest of their lives due to being too dangerous for society. Then there are those whose dreams and aspirations were never to end up in prison, but due to many factors in their life, that's where they end up. It's such a true saying to 'never judge a book by its cover.' We all have the potential to one day be a prisoner and with this as a starting point, you will do well.

Life is about balance. I have said throughout this chapter that there good and bad in every job. One of the best things is to always keep an open mind and a sense of humour. Do not take ourselves too seriously. There are many teachable moments as we go through life. Prison staff taught me to trust and that not everyone is the same. I taught them that we are human and certainly more than a number. Prison officers need a sense of humour. Having a relationship goes a long way with a prison officer. I remember one prison officer, Ted. In Scotland there is big football rivalry between Celtic and Rangers. Ted, bless him was born into a Rangers jersey. I was born into Paradise Celtic FC myself. Ted and I would make jokes at each other when old firm games were on. Ted would come into my cell to watch the match and we would constantly rip into each other; Rangers fans use a term 1690 to do with King Billy and protestant jargon. Ted would shout me by shouting '1690.' I would respond to him, and other inmates thought this was my prison number.

Inmates would say 'what a fucking jail number to be given to a Celtic man.' I would then let them know it wasn't my number. It was just Ted at his best. My point to this is that through our relationship we didn't take ourselves seriously. We used humour, banter, pater, and this brought joy and laughter throughout the day when I needed it most. Days when I was down and in low mood. It was the Good Prison Officer who came and wound me up a bit and got me laughing because we had a relationship. In any context, we should never underestimate the power of the relationships and connections.

When I was moved to the open estate, I had to say goodbye to the staff. I never got to say goodbye to all staff due to shift changes and Ted was one of them. In the open estate you would receive external mail (family) and internal mail (social workers and addiction workers etc). I see on the board I have internal mail; I go up to collect it and on the envelope was 1690. I burst out laughing. Ted had given the bus that was bringing up the next intake from closed conditions a letter for me. Inside was a letter and he is wishing me well on my journey and hoping that Ted *never* sees me again on the inside. I genuinely had tears of joy as I read through his kind words and support. Of course, at the end he signed it off with 'Fuck the Celtic.' What a man!

I did meet Ted again out shopping with my mother. I introduced Ted to my mother as a friend from prison. She asked what sentence he had done. I responded with 26 years as a prison officer and a good one at that! The importance of relationships in every aspect of our lives is fundamental. As prison officers, you may be the one who plants the seed or makes the connection. Just to listen, treat people as people and with respect. If Mark never made that intervention, I don't know where I would be today. Mark, Ted, and others unconsciously built a foundation in me while I was in prison and probably gave me the trust-to-trust others. I went on my journey through rehab and to where I am today. There have been many important people who have all supported me since leaving prison. However, the intervention, the relationships with staff in the prison gave me enough to move on so much.

Today, I work with police, schools' teachers, prison staff, social workers, and government. I was seen as a person at the end and not a number. As a prison officer you are more than the uniform. You're a human, a son, a daughter, a brother, sister, father, mother. We will never be perfect at our jobs. However, we can work towards perfecting our relationships with others. When you go home after a shift with peace of mind knowing that you done the best that you can, just by listening, chatting, being there looking beyond the behaviour of others, and seeing the human side. This is when you have become, *The Good Prison Officer.*

The person who holds the key to another person's freedom is the person who needs kindness, compassion, and care for others as they are the beholders that can unlock the potential in another person.

EVERY ACT OF KINDNESS LEAVES A TRACE!

References

Binswanger, I. A., Nowels, C., Corsi, K. F. *et al.* (2012) Return to drug use and overdose after release from prison: a qualitative study of risk and protective factors. *Addiction Science & Clinical Practice*, 7, 3. https://doi.org/10.1186/1940-0640-7-3

Brierley. A., (2019). *Your honour can I tell you my story.* Waterside Press.

Buck, G. (2018). The core conditions of peer mentoring. *Criminology & Criminal Justice*, *18*(2), 190–206.

Campbell, C. A., Albert, I., Jarrett, M., Byrne, M., Roberts, A., Phillip, P., & Valmaggia, L. (2016). Treating multiple incident post-traumatic stress disorder (PTSD) in an inner city London prison: The need for an evidence base. *Behavioural and Cognitive Psychotherapy*, *44*(1), 112–117.

Engel, G. L. (1981). The clinical application of the biopsychosocial model. *The Journal of Medicine and Philosophy: A Forum for Bioethics and Philosophy of Medicine*, *6*(2), 101–124.

Farrell, M., & Marsden, J. (2008). Acute risk of drug-related death among newly released prisoners in England and Wales. *Addiction*, *103*(2), 25.

Farrington, D. P. (2005). Childhood origins of antisocial behavior. Clinical Psychology & Psychotherapy: An International Journal of Theory & Practice, 12(3), 177–190.

Felitti, V. J., Anda, R. F., Nordenberg, D., Williamson, D. F., Spitz, A. M., Edwards, V., & Marks, J. S. (1998). Relationship of childhood abuse and household dysfunction to many of the leading causes of death in adults: The adverse childhood experiences (ACE) study. *American Journal of Preventive Medicine*, *14*(4), 245–258.

Fry, D., Fang, X., Elliott, S., Casey, T., Zheng, X., Li, J., & McCluskey, G. (2018). The relationships between violence in childhood and educational outcomes: A global systematic review and meta-analysis. *Child Abuse & Neglect*, *75*, 6–28.

Hudson, K., Maguire, M., & Raynor, P. (2012). Through the prison gate: Resettlement, offender management and the 'seamless sentence'. In *Handbook on prisons* (pp. 659–679). Routledge.

Maté, G. (2012). Addiction: Childhood trauma, stress and the biology of addiction. *Journal of Restorative Medicine*, *1*(1), 56–63.

Weaver, A. (2008). So You Think You Know Me? Waterside Press.

Winfrey, O., & Perry, B. D. (2021). *What happened to you?: Conversations on trauma, resilience, and healing.* Flatiron Books.

4 Flexibility: Negotiation and Discretion

Max Dennehy, Prison Number - A3090CK

Who Am I?

I am Max, a 33-year-old father to two beautiful daughters and partner to a beautiful woman. I work for a third-sector addiction and recovery charity as a 'Recovery Housing Support Worker.' This involves working with people in the community and in housing, and walking together, shoulder to shoulder, through their journey. I have lived experience of both addiction and recovery, and I use my experiences to connect with our residents on a level that they understand. I look and sound like them; *I am them* – only a few years in the future. I try, as much as possible, to remove the hierarchical or sometimes paternalistic nature of services. Although similar to a topic I broach in this chapter, it sometimes rests on a knife edge of what is and isn't permissible when trying to connect with people on a level that they will respond, while simultaneously maintaining professional boundaries when working alongside vulnerable people. I am also studying Criminology and Sociology at Lancaster University. I was excluded from school and gained my qualification to get into university on an ACCESS: higher education (HE) course in 2019 at the age of 30. HE is something that I have come to love, and something that I have found difficult, at times, to navigate, both logistically – having a young family and work commitments – and emotionally. The university can feel intimidating and hostile when you're from my background. However, this is getting easier over time.

I entered a residential rehab in 2018 after 15 years of addiction. I started taking drugs and alcohol in my early teens and progressed to heroin at the age of 16. My life was chaotic enough before. However, from 16 onwards, it's been a serious rollercoaster. My addiction to drugs and alcohol has seen me on the revolving door of police, probation, and prison. I have done things that I wouldn't do again today, some things

DOI: 10.4324/9781003349747-4

I am not proud of. However, coming into recovery, the biggest lesson I learnt was that 'I am not the person that I thought I was.' I used to believe that I was the total sum of my actions. I believed that life on the margins, battling with addiction and dysfunction, was how people like me should live. I didn't know that something else was out there for me – something in touching distance. A life beyond my wildest dreams. I have lost many friends to drugs and suicide over the years, and I have people still out in the madness. My hope is that if I can combine my experience with education, I can try to reach the people who, like once was the case for me, can't see a way out because no one has ever shown it to them. There are two worlds: there is the marginalised and excluded – and there's everyone else. As scholars, professionals, and community members, we must do what we can to bridge the gap between the two.

My Prison Experience

The title of this book is *The Good Prison Officer: Inside Perspectives*. This is precisely what I have – a perspective. My prison experiences took place in a Local Category B prison, and in sentenced category C prisons. I have had consistent contact with the criminal justice system since aged 15. My sentences (time served) ranged from six months to two years over four separate sentences, until my last sentence in 2016. It is important for me to outline this when talking about my perspective as I am aware that my experience, and therefore understanding, is concentrated in specific places, in specific locations, at a specific time. My understanding of prison, my role in prison, the role of other prisoners, and the role of the staff, as I communicate to you in my writing, is done so with the fortune of hindsight, deep reflection, and continuous learning. I did not know then what I know today, and I use this as a tool to apply to and unpick my past. My experiences of prison and prison life were complex and multi-faceted. However, for the purpose of this chapter, I will concentrate on the register of my experience that works best with the aims of this book – to provide an 'inside perspective' that may help and somewhat improve understanding and subsequently practice among prison officers.

My experience of prison living is one of chronic stress, hypervigilance, and performance. A jarring combination of 'banter,' 'toy-fighting,' 'shit-talking,' and 'grafting,' alongside hostility, violence, high anxiety, and a relentless interpretation and assessment of everything and everybody around me. Existing in a state of high stress and hypervigilance is something I brought in from the outside. Coming from the streets and being involved in the world of drug addiction and crime involves living in close proximity to violence, danger, risk-taking behaviours, and unpredictability (see McGarvey, 2019). However, and arguably so, on the outside, there are, or at least *can be*, intermittent breaks from this state. Whether it be geographical space such as particular houses, areas, or settings; whether it be relational; or whether it be the relief that drugs and alcohol provide to self-soothe from pains of living in this heightened and aggressive state – there was, at times, for me at least, an escape from the consuming toxic stress and hyper-vigilance (see Bucci et al., 2016). I would describe being in prison as being a reproduction of the same core conditions – such as anxiety, stress, and hyper-vigilance - that come as part of being in the streets on the outside – only tenfold.

Daily life and interactions in prison are steeped in performance and scrutiny (see Maguire, 2021). That is not to say that interactions are false and disingenuous; moreover, how we conduct ourselves and perform in jail is important and conveys to others the message that we are trying to communicate about ourselves. Similarly, the scrutiny of others' performances is a necessary act of information gathering and self-preservation. Take, for example, what may seem like a benign and unassuming conversation that is commonplace in jail – especially in local jails – 'where are you from? what are you in for?' In my experience, from both sides of the conversation, this line of questioning is a process of assessment and evaluation. Each of the questions spurs follow-up questions – 'who do you know? how many jail sentences have you done? which prisons have you been in? what was the offence? how long did you get? did you get remanded? why didn't you get bail' etc. – this conversation, however friendly, or not, it may seem, is essential for a prisoner to establish their legitimacy and authenticity. Similarly, it is an opportunity for the questioner to scrutinise and pull apart answers, explore discrepancies, and form some sort of judgement on the character of the person.

This information is vital to assess the potential that a person carries – the potential to change the dynamic of a wing, the threat that a person may pose, the potential to be carrying drugs, be a 'grass' or a 'nonce.' In addition to simply answering the questions, much of a prisoner's authenticity and legitimacy as a 'proper prisoner' in these interactions also rests on the performance, or style, of the communication. For example, the type of words used, the body language displayed, the person's posture, the way they carry themselves, and hold up under pressure – all this information is used to build up a picture. I use these interactions as an example of how intense, multi-layered, and dynamic everyday prison interactions can be. Therefore, I found, that the use and utilisation of space and interactions in prison played a significant role in providing brief respite from the intensity.

Sociologist Erving Goffman (1990) conceptualised everyday inter-actions in his work 'Presenting the everyday self' as a 'Dramaturgy.' Goffman (1990) surmised that individuals work through everyday life much in the same way an actor would treat a staged performance, with specific roles, scripts, and performances suited to particular scenes and settings. Goffman (1990) specifically noted the difference and distinc-tion between individuals, or 'actors', whenever they are occupying, what he describes as either a 'front stage' space or a 'backstage' space. Goffman (1990) uses many examples to show how individuals engaged in the performance of how a role can switch between the 'front stage' and 'backstage.' One of the examples used is that of the waiter in a fancy restaurant. The 'frontstage' space for the waiter would be the restau-rant floor. In this space, the waiter would be engaged in a performance that requires him or her to give off the appearance of sophistication, elegance, and politeness to his or her audience. However, when the waiter moves from the restaurant floor into the kitchen space – the 'backstage' space – this performance can be dropped, and a waiter may be rushing, shouting, swearing, organising, or regrouping. It is in the backstage that the messy business of the maintenance of the frontstage performance is carried out.

'The performance of an individual in a front region may be seen as an effort to give the appearance that his activity in the region maintains and embodies certain standards' (Goffman, 1990, p. 110). In the prison context, the space that resembles Goffman's front stage is the space that exists within the forward-facing sanctioned regime of the prison, the prison landings, association, phone queues, showers, movement, the servery etc. These spaces of vulnerability require navigation, a height-ened state of stress, and an over-exposure to scrutiny. When describing the backstage, Goffman (1990, p. 115) states, '…here the performer can relax; he [sic] can drop his front, forgo his speaking lines, and step out of character.' For me, the cell was the most obvious form of backstage space – a space that provided respite from the chronic stress and relent-less hyper-vigilance of prison life.

Sometimes, when the cell door would bang shut behind me at the end of the day, I would breathe a sigh of relief; I would let go of some of the weight that came with carrying on a performance under relentless surveillance and scrutiny whilst, similarly, scrutinising and interpreting each and everything around me. The door would shut, and the day was done. The trials and tribulations and the intensity of the politics of everyday life on the prison landings were paused – if only for 12 hours. In this space, I felt I could let go and resume a sense of normalcy. It would allow space for me to de-brief the day's events with my pad-mate, draw up plans for the next day ahead, daydream about the future, listen to music, watch the soaps, and wait for a film to come on. We would talk for hours, sit in silence, and ponder. In this space, I could, to some degree, re-engage with some level of rational thought and hold a space that allowed for humanity.

I understand that 'the cell' as a backstage space, a place of comfort and respite, is not a universal experience amongst prisoners. In fact, depending upon a plethora of different moving parts and conditions, 'the cell' may be a place for someone for extreme discomfort and potential violence. I outline the cell as a potential backstage space because I believe the 'backstage' semi-therapeutic conditions in the cell can be and *is*, on some level, reproduced within what would nor-mally be considered the 'front stage' of prison. '…still there are many regions which function at one time and in one sense as a front region and at another time and in another sense as a back region' (Goffman, 1990, p. 127). It is my experience that spaces can exist inside within the forward-facing prison regime that can provide brief and intermit-ted pockets of space that replicate the conditions that I found to be helpful from within the cell.

Prison scholars Crewe et al. (2014) highlight the importance of space inside the prison in their article on 'the emotional geography of prison life.' Crewe et al. (2014) discuss how different spaces and settings within the prison's internal geography can promote or sup-press moments of emotional vulnerability. However, when referencing Goffman (1990) and the 'front and backstage' analogy, Crewe et al. (2014, p. 59) offer that this '…does not seem entirely adequate' due to the '…binary description of "front" and "back" stages, or private and public domains.' Although the point that Crewe et al. (2014) makes has validity – I think that as a whole this illuminates the nuance and com-plexity of how space can be used and repurposed. Crewe et al. (2014) point to spaces that I would consider as being separated from the sharp front of the regime that exists and dominates within the wings and landings; spaces such as education, workshops, and the visiting room. Whilst I agree with the totality of the article, and if the subject matter of this chapter is of interest to you, I would recommend reading it – I do have a different understanding of how space can be fluid enough to provide front and backstage functions almost simultaneously.

My argument is that, yes, whilst it is definitely harder to recreate the unique qualities that those spaces provide away from the landings, there is, in my opinion, a definite potential in recreating 'backstage' spaces on the landings, on the wings – in the 'frontstage' – through prisoners and officers working collaboratively in utilising flexibility, discretion and negotiation with the rules. My understanding through my experience is that 'backstage' space can be carved out, co-opted, and repurposed from within the sanctioned regime, that allow for moments, however fleeting, of recess, mitigation, and release from the repressive and oppressive conditions of everyday prison life and everyday prison interactions. Sometimes, whilst not being in education or employment, as the officers in the morning or afternoon unlocked the cell doors for work or education, I would use the opportunity of the open door to leave the cell and get out onto the landings. I would go and talk to friends through the doors, hang around, and socialise – mingle, whilst the rest of the wing went off on programmes. Often, my aim in this was to stay out long enough to be still on the landings when the officers shut the doors again for morning or afternoon bang up.

This is obviously against the rules and outside of what is sanctioned by the prison regime; therefore, it would often require me to 'blend it' – a process involving a combination of hiding, movement, and giving the appearance of being involved in something meaningful. I remember a period when my friend Tommy was in the middle of running a heavy trial that, in the end, saw him getting life imprisonment. Tommy was 'padded up' with a wing cleaner so his door was open during work. I would get out for the morning through my tactics, and we would talk about where he was at, how he was feeling, his worries for the future. When everyone was around Tommy acted like he didn't care and was always being a joker – it was in these moments that me and Tommy could drop the front for thirty minutes or so and be 'real.'

Being out of my cell during a time when everyone who was not engaged with work or education should have been 'banged up' – is obviously against the rules. However, there has been plenty of times, and not just for myself – for other prisoners too – that a prison officer has seen me out of the cell and on the landings at these times and not acted. The officer may have given me a 'nod' or a cue to let me know that they know I am out of the cell; they may have pretended to have not seen me, or I may have blatantly asked to be out – 'Gov, can you open me up, so I clean my pad out.' This involves an underenforcement of the sanctioned regime and therefore requires the use of flexibility, discretion, and negotiation on the part of the prison officer. The Good Prison Officers understand how to manage this level of negation which maintains legitimacy and also their ability to maintain security and control.

Advice from the Inside

Prison scholar Alison Liebling (2000) writes about the use of negotiation and discretion in the policing of prisons by prison officers. Liebling (2000) lays out (see also Hepburn, 1985) six power bases used by officers in prison. One of these power bases is 'exchange power – the informal reward system: underenforcement and accommodation' (Liebling, 2000, p. 341). Negotiation and discretion, in my experience – although I have highlighted the co-opting and repurposing of space as being vital for creating semi-therapeutic pockets of space – is used in the same manner and to much the same effect, similarly, in the minutia of everyday interactions. For example, when the call 'that's it lads, behind your doors thank you' reverberates around the wing at the end of association, and the hustle and bustle steps up a notch; as people fly around 'grafting,' 'hustling,' and tying up loose ends to ensure that they are going behind the door with what they need to get through the night – food, coffee, sugar, tobacco (pre-smoking ban) etc. – on numerous occasions I have requested to the officer 'gov, listen, I just need to run down to X to grab X – gimme two secs' and have been given a subtle nod and gone off to sort out loose ends quickly. The same can be said for finishing off in the showers or many different routine activities. Liebling (2000, p. 343) found that, on the ground, prison officers often understood that 'the decent thing' is selectively to underenforce the law, in order that the smooth flow of prison can continue (see also Sykes, 1958). However, the opposite has also been true. There were times that I needed to 'grab something back' from someone – grab some rizla, or tuna, or noodles, get an ordinary letter (O/L) from the office etc. – an officer has not been interested in engaging in this process and has denied these requests and 'banged up' regardless.

Now, I understand that the end of association is the end of association, and if I had my way, I would have been running around the landing all night! However, there does need to be some degree of flexibility and movement when it comes to working with people. This way of thinking is commonly accepted in other walks of life outside of the prison. However, when it comes to prisoners, it can be easy to deny our humanity and forget the struggles of what it is to live behind a locked door. In reality, what it means to go *behind the door* without sugar for a cup of tea, the book you wanted to borrow, the paper you wanted to use to write a letter, the sauce that you lent to someone for the sandwich you saved, the rizla, or lighter, or tobacco that you needed to be able to have smoke at night (pre-smoking ban) is to completely rob a person of their agency, autonomy, sense of dignity, and humanity.

I will never forget one of the nights I had gone behind the door with tobacco and no lighter. I had just come back in after only being out for six weeks, and my head was not in a great place. I was withdrawing from the drugs I had been taking whilst outside. I tried in different ways to get myself a 'wick and wheel' (a homemade lighting device using flint and thread) by sending 'lines' (threads and ripped bedsheet sheets that are thrown out from under the door to other cells to create a 'line') but to no avail. I 'got on the buzzer', and to my surprise, the 'night clocker' came and was helpful − he couldn't get a lighter to me; however, he did agree to light my cigarette through the crack in the door, and he came back round every hour all night (and I was up all night) and lit my cigarette.

I am sure that the officer doing that would not be within the rules of the prison, except at that moment, he saw my humanity and made a choice. I do not know that night clocker's name, and I don't remember his face − however, I will remember that night for the rest of my life. My point is that, through flexibility, backstage space can be created − a space of respite, release, and humanity. Whether it be geographical pockets of space and time on the landings and on the wings, or whether it be in the interaction between officer and prisoner, through using negotiation and discretion, it is possible to get behind the sharp front of prison life and into a space that can create a shield, if only momentarily, from the unhealthy levels of toxic stress that are related to chronic hyper-vigilance, relentless performance and surveillance. Over exposure to toxic stress in childhood has been shown to have long lasting negative health effects on the human body throughout the life course of human development (Shonkoff et al., 2012). Therefore, over exposure to such stressors within the context of custody for adults that have been disproportionally exposed to poverty, stigma, social exclusion, addiction, racism, or abuse and neglect as outlined earlier by Brierley, backstage spaces are not only a necessity for respite, they are also imperative for the mind, body, and soul to recover, heal, and repair.

Although I am advocating for the use of flexibility, negotiation, and discretion in order to carve out backstage spaces from within the sanctioned regime, there is, however, a crux; not all prisoners are always acting in good faith, myself, at times, included. Therefore, the judgement calls to allow an individual some extra time to carry out an activity or to enable an individual to be operating in a space, even briefly, outside of the sanctioned regime can carry the potential to develop into harmful activity − activity such as violence, harmful drug taking, bullying behaviour. However, this being said, the reasons behind prisoners 'trying their luck' or 'grafting' is often genuine. 'Grafting' has many meanings. The original definition of 'graft' is 'hard-work.' Another meaning for 'graft' is to steal, rob, and be involved in acquisitive criminal activity. 'Grafting' can mean selling drugs, and, in the context that I am using it, 'grafting' can mean to manipulate – to work a person for an intended outcome. It may be off-putting to prison officers that even when a prison officer is fluent in exercising flexible authority and is seen as legitimate, often, the interaction in which discretion and negotiation can be applied can be framed as a 'graft' or being 'grafted.' I would use that language without even thinking... 'yeah, I'll just graft Mr Roberts to open me up and clean my pad.' However, this is nothing personal. As I alluded to earlier, the vantage point of waking up every morning locked behind a steel door with no access to *genuine* autonomy and *genuine* agency means that every day is a hustle – and to hustle, you need to 'graft.'

The choice between when to exercise discretion and when to stay firm – when to selectively underenforce and when not to – must be tough (Crewe, 2011). An overenforcement of the rules and regime can be interpreted as coercive and overly authoritarian as outlined in Andi Brierley's chapter regarding the varying levels of power used by officers. An underenforcement of the rules allows chaos, confusion, and dramatically effects safety on the wings (Crewe et al., 2015). Both these positions would render an officer, to me at least, as illegitimate, unworthy of respect – and therefore lacking in legitimate authority (see Liebling, 2011; Steiner & Wooldredge, 2018). The complexity and nuance of prison life is deep and dynamic. The ability to receive and interpret the subtleties of prison life, the ability to 'read the room' and navigate space in prison requires a high level of emotional intelligence and understanding of the environment. As I mentioned earlier, as a prisoner, like many others, coming into the prison after years of navigating similar situations on the outside, I was able to adjust quickly after being provided, effectively, years of training on the outside to be able to carry this out. I can only imagine for a prison officer; this must take years to tune in.

The Chief Inspector of Prisons has recently stated that recruitment and staff retention is the 'biggest work on the horizon' for the Prison Service (Inside Times, 2022). According to the Ministry of Justice (2022), 2021 saw a record number of resignations, with more than 200 permanent officers resigning from permanent positions between August and September. This is, however, now a chronic feature of the prison service, with 1 in 9 officers leaving the service every year compared to 1 in 25 a decade ago (Inside Times, 2022). For all the concerns and criticism that have been laid at the feet of the 'old guard' cohort of prison officers, valid as they may be, there was a quality about these officers, related to the length of time spent working in the prison, that cannot be reproduced in a short amount of time.

I am not claiming that some of these officers were without fault, or that what I am describing can be universally applied across the whole group – far from it. However, what I saw was a dramatic decrease in the amount of understanding and experience on the landings that hurt the prison. Many of these officers came from the same communities that we came from, had watched us grow up and go through trials and tribulations. Many of these officers had spent more time in prison than we had. These experiences of navigating such spaces for long periods of time meant that many officers were just as 'tapped' as us! With this comes an air of legitimacy that cannot be synthesised and reproduced. In my experience, some of the newer, younger, and less experienced officers would either under-enforce the rules and regime and garner no legitimacy at all, be seen as 'wet behind the ears,' or they would overcorrect and over-enforce (see Crewe et al., 2015), not allow for any discretion and flexibility which, I would assert, is just as harmful – not only because of the reasons I have outlined regarding space and moments away from the repression of the regime and conditions of toxic stress, but because, although prison is at its core coercive, in order for a wing to run safely and smoothly there must be some degree of 'consent.'

A prison is a stressful place. Navigating space while enduring conditions of toxic stress – hyper-vigilance, performance, surveillance, and scrutiny – can be exhausting and detrimental to an environment that could potentially provide an opportunity for reflection and healing. During my time, I found that there can be brief pockets of space – intermittent respite – created through interaction and the repurposing of space. Goffman's work on front and backstage provides a framework to conceptualise the different ways we occupy and navigate spaces in different ways. The front and backstage are not relegated to the cell's privacy and the landings' exposure; there can be spaces and moments carved out of the forward-facing regime. However, this requires prison officers to be, to some degree, flexible; to deploy tactics of negotiation and discretion. Getting the balance of this is challenging and by no means an easy feat and therefore requires a level of emotional intelligence, authority, and legitimacy that is not easily earned in prison. Thus, the poor staff retention rate as outlined by HMPPS is, undoubtably, a problem. I am not condemning and writing off the new staff that go into the prison service; moreover, I am highlighting just how important it is to have people in the job who understand, almost intuitively,

the complexity, the dynamics, and the nuance of everyday prison life —
this is something that comes with time, training, and education and
increases the likelihood of being that *Good Prison Officer.*

References

Bucci, M., Marques, S. S., Oh, D., & Harris, N. B. (2016). Toxic stress in children
and adolescents. *Advances in Pediatrics, 63*(1), 403–428.

Crewe, B. (2011). Soft power in prison: Implications for staff–prisoner relationships, liberty and legitimacy. *European Journal of Criminology, 8*(6), 455–468.

Crewe, B., Liebling, A., & Hulley, S. (2015). Staff-prisoner relationships, staff professionalism, and the use of authority in public-and private-sector prisons. *Law
& Social Inquiry, 40*(2), 309–344.

Crewe, B., Warr, J., Bennett, P., & Smith, A. (2014). The emotional geography of
prison life. *Theoretical Criminology, 18*(1), 56–74.

Goffman, E. (1990 [1959]). *The presentation of self in everyday life.* Penguin.

Hepburn, J. R. (1985). The exercise of power in coercive organizations: A study of
prison guards. *Criminology, 23*(1), 145–164.

Inside Times. (2022). Chief inspector warns on prison officer shortage. *Inside Times*
[online]. Retrieved 13 August 2022, from https://insidetime.org/chief-inspector-
warns-on-prison-officer-shortage/

Liebling, A. (2000). Prison officers, policing and the use of discretion. *Theoretical
Criminology, 4*(3), 333–357.

Liebling, A. (2011). Distinctions and distinctiveness in the work of prison officers:
Legitimacy and authority revisited. *European Journal of Criminology, 8*(6), 484–499.

Maguire, D. (2021). *Male, failed, jailed: Masculinities and 'revolving door' imprisonment
in the UK.* Springer International Publishing.

McGarvey, D. (2019). *Poverty safari.* Rizzoli.

Shonkoff, J. P., Garner, A. S., Siegel, B. S., Dobbins, M. I., Earls, M. F., & McGuinn,
L. (2012). The lifelong effects of early childhood adversity and toxic stress.
Pediatrics, 129(1), e232–e246.

Steiner, B., & Wooldredge, J. (2018). Prison officer legitimacy, their exercise of
power, and inmate rule breaking. *Criminology, 56*(4), 750–779.

Sykes, G. M. (2007 [1958]). *The society of captives: A study of a maximum security
prison.* Princeton University Press.

5 I Have Never Met a Child That Healed in a Cell

Kierra Myles, Prison Number - 28447

Who Am I?

Hey, I'm Kierra Myles. I am 33 years old and a mummy to an amazing 8-year-old son. I am also a daughter, granddaughter, aunty, niece, and friend. I love the beach, the sea, and spending time connecting with nature. I have a purple belt in Brazilian Jiujitsu and compete as often as I can! I train in different martial arts and lift the odd weight; training is very important because it keeps me grounded and connected to myself. I work as a Mentor Co-ordinator with children in care and care leavers, predominately involved in the youth justice system.

I feel blessed to work within a role that focuses on building trusting relationships with young people and supporting them to navigate through the care and justice system. Empowering them to have a say in their lives and build further relationships creates secure attachments. Research suggests that supporting someone to transition from one space to another, in this instance to move away from the criminal justice system and the associated behaviours, that it is not necessarily the tools or programmes, but rather the existence of trusting, empathic, and consistent relationships between children and professional adults (France & Homel, 2006).

A massive part of my role as a Mentor Co-ordinator is that I don't have an agenda, only to be there for children and young people when they need me. For them to allow me to be there when they need me requires me to have an established trusting relationship with children and young people in trouble (Brierley, 2021). Building a relationship takes time, and requires flexibility and a compassionate approach. Children and young people in trouble often come from a background of trauma with a high number of adverse childhood experiences (Felitti et al., 1998). Research suggests many children that enter the youth justice system have suffered exclusion, poor housing, and

DOI: 10.4324/9781003349747-5

poverty. They are often further traumatised by their own behaviours and responses to their environment and the trauma they have suffered, such as serious youth violence (Gray et al., 2021)). The last thing traumatised children need is another know it all professional from afar coming along and trying to tell them how to change to obtain a better life. After all, it's not programmes that help children recover from trauma; it's the relationships we have with people (Hambrick et al., 2019; Perry, 2007; Perry & Szalavitz, 2017).

Through relationship-based practice in youth justice, as well as a continuous honest reflection of my own practice, I have been able to build some amazing relationships with young people who have found it difficult to trust the adults and services around them. It's only through trust and hope that they felt able and empowered to speak up for themselves, have a say in their lives, and get involved in participation and co-production (Creaney & Case, 2020; Smithson & Jones, 2021). I mean, if we want to see services improve for the better, we must listen to those who are living the experience now, right? I have managed to build solid, trusting relationships with partner agencies and the voluntary sector. Coming together as professionals to support the people we are trying to help create better lives is very important if we want those, we are supporting to have the best chances of success, keeping them at the centre of decision making.

In my experience, people who transit through the desistance process capitalising on both functionality and capability do not necessarily change who they are as a person. Therefore, we must be careful with the word *change*. People that desist from offending often change the way they view people, the world around them, their behaviour, friends, and family. However, they don't really change who they are as people. They very rarely swap sides and comply with the system and its messages, so this shouldn't be the focus of justice professionals. The idea that children and young people must change who they are is scary and pushes them away. It's like telling someone who they are at their very core is bad, shameful, and should have no part of their future. To inspire change in someone that's been in prison to move away from the behaviours that got them there, they must first be able to see another way. That they have hope and belief that they can achieve hope beyond the pains of custody and criminality. Often children and young people cannot see a different way. Children I have had the privilege of working with are in care or leaving care. These care experiences are not because their lives have been happy, filled with love, trusting relationships, and safety. This lack of relational attachments that we as humans need to be well is described as relational poverty from both lived experience and literature (Brierley 2021; Hambrick et al., 2019a).

Through my work as a front-line practitioner, mentoring, advocating, and most importantly listening to young people, my senior managers have started to recognise the impact of having a relationship with someone who has shared experiences, especially with children and young people involved in serious youth violence, drug dealing, and what could be considered gang crime. I have recently been given the opportunity to create a peer mentor team of people with care experience. I have spent the last year or so speaking to as many people as possible, gathering information, data, and building relationships across services all over the UK and Scotland to create a plan that means peer mentors will be paid workers and not volunteers! This project is in its infancy, but it is a project that I am very excited about. Having someone who has been where you are and managed to navigate the way out and lead a happy and relatively normal life is invaluable. It's not what those with lived experience say it's all the things they don't say, the way they hold themselves, the way they feel and empathise that helps develop trust, redressing the power dynamic.

We know that children in care are overrepresented in the youth justice system (Laming, 2016). Claire Fitzpatrick et al. (2022) found that girls were not being diverted from the criminal justice system; they were often being criminalised because a 'one size fits all' approach was taken. The aim of peer mentoring is to provide a relationship based on the needs to the child; it's not necessarily about diverting children from the criminal justice system. However, we know that if children do not have anyone, they can trust and no safe relationships they are extremely vulnerable to exploitation. Peer mentoring for children in care and care leavers involved in justice services is an alternative child-centred way of putting relationships at the centre of practice. Peer mentors are often seen as a source of inspiration and hope that life can be better even for people that come from their social position, not just other people. A recognition that it does not have to be like this forever. They often connect with people who have similar shared experiences, finding comfort in this shared identity and spending time with others who have similar identities and experiences that the justice system spends a lot of time trying to change. A welcoming space with no judgement, shame, or expectation attached to it. 'Mentors who are current or former offenders who have overcome adversity, for instance emotional distress pain and suffering, can be perceived by mentees as positive role models and a source of hope' (Creaney 2020, p. 25).

My Prison Experience

I guess you could say that my prison experience is unique. I entered HMP La Moye at 15 years old. I was on the adult female wing in a young offender's cell. I remember going there in the van. I was given a 4-month prison sentence for not complying with my community service order. I mean, I had barely attended secondary school and they were expecting me to work for free as punishment, as if. I would describe this as setting a child up to fail. If deterrence and punishment worked, school would have been a safe place for me, but it wasn't because I felt judged for my lack of attention and ability to deal with structure and boundaries which is a response to my childhood experiences.

Let's go back a bit though to explain. We know that children did not end up in custody because everything was going well in their lives. I was born into childhood trauma. We lived in a flat where I shared a room with my older brother. My home was filled with anger and addiction, with different people coming and going. To be honest, I don't remember all that much before I was 7 years old. I remember having to wear extra clothes because it was so cold, and we couldn't afford the heating. I remember not having much food in my lunchbox, stealing sweets from the shop, and the long walks in the rain because my mum didn't drive. She used to walk so fast, we had to keep up, otherwise we'd be in trouble. I remember my body holding all the hurt and pain; sometimes as a small child, I would hide in the corner. It was like a place of comfort; I don't remember any long-term safe people in my life as a child. Feeling safe with other human beings is fundamental to developing secure attachments and leading a healthy life (Van Der Kolk, 2014).

My dad was an alcoholic. He was around while I was a baby on and off until he went to rehab when I was three. He has maintained sobriety since, one day at a time. Initially, my mum made it quite difficult for him to see me. However, he was the only consistent person I had during my teenage years. No matter where I lived, he would always show up when he told me he would. I saw him weekly most of the time. I remember living with him for a while when I was 11 before I went into care because he also couldn't cope with me getting in trouble, disappearing, and being unable to manage my emotions. There were times that I would be suspended from school, and in his flat, there would only be some bread, milk, and butter in the house; he would turn the electricity off at the mains so I couldn't watch TV. He tried his best with the resources available to him; the issue was most of the relational damage and childhood trauma had already permeated my mind, body, and soul.

Both my parents came from a background of trauma, making the experience cyclical. My dad went to prison as a child and my mum's dad committed suicide when mum was three years old. They also grew up in homes where they were fearful. The adults around them were unpredictable, leaving them growing up in a household of uncertainty. We understand that children need predictable and stable attachments to develop well, and parents that had traumatic or challenging childhoods often struggle with their own infants (Cicchetti et al., 2006). Neither of them had properly developed the skills they needed to raise children by the time they had children. My dad was more nurturing by nature because of his childhood, whereas my mum was angry by nature. My mum went to work when we were young and taught us work ethic and manners. My dad would take me fishing, and we would watch sports. He would show up to my football games.

I was first excluded from school at just 8 years old. I was further excluded and moved around to another eight schools, which included education in custody. My teachers always said I was a bright child. However, they also labelled me as oppositional, aggressive, and violent. I did not like being told what to do due to my childhood of unpredict-able and chaotic relational environments. I often reacted negatively to situations that pushed me outside my window of tolerance, leaving me emotionally vulnerable without the tools or understanding of how to respond. This was not 'only in response to threatening events but also to their anticipation' (Corrigan et al., 2011, p. 19). I hadn't developed the ability to manage situations that challenged me. I did not receive the consistent and predictable relationships a child needs to develop attachments to other humans and learn how to emotionally regulate. My stress response was overreactive. This means my stress response was like a little alarm ringing at the back of my head constantly searching for threats and signs of harm coming my way. Sometimes there was harm, and sometimes, the threat was long gone or even just inaccu-rately assessed on my behalf. I would be triggered into a trauma-based response when I expected a challenge. Still with no safe, reliable, and predictable adult, I did not have the ability to understand why I kept reacting in ways I had little control over. This will be the case for many prisoners in your care.

When I was 11, I was arrested for shoplifting; some boys 4–5 years older than me would tell me which CDs to get; I thought I was good at it until I got caught! I loved going in there with the CD orders, man the adrenaline. I had respect from the older boys, although I was a girl, I was a tom boy; I played football, and due to my homelife, I was tough. I wasn't scared of confrontation, and I just wanted to be accepted. At

12, I went into care, a 12-bedroom children's home. One of my friends went to foster care; I remember going around the house and wondering why I wasn't allowed to go to foster care. I was living in a large house that I did not want to be in, so I did what you'd expect a 12-year-old child who has a history of continuous trauma to do; I ran away.

I first entered custody at 13 years old; I was remanded to a secure children's home for a month. I was in and out of that place for the next two years while being moved between two 12-bedroom children's homes, my dad's, and my mums. I did not know what stability was. I had to be about my wits; I had to read people and rooms in seconds because my life depended on it. I still had this overactive stress response that would not let me rest. There was a constant alarm ringing in my head, searching for danger and threats; it was exhausting. The secure home made it worse. There were more unreliable, unpredictable adults that were supposed to be caring for me instead, they were slamming my face into the floor and restraining me because they didn't support me to reduce my anxiety levels.

When I first went to HMP at 15 years old. I remember going into my cell. It had a metal bed, thin mattress, and a wardrobe. The place I came from recently had a wooden bedframe and chair built into it. Before that, it was a bare cell with just a crash mat on the floor. When I didn't comply with the demands of the secure home, or should I say when I didn't respond well to coercive control, they would take the crash mat out during school hours, leaving me to sit on the cold floor. This HMP cell was like a luxury in comparison. I was told it would be much worse. I was always warned of stories from professionals about how bad it would be if I went to adult prison. It would be much worse than anywhere I'd been before. It was quite the opposite. It was the best place I have lived in my life to this point. It became the longest I had stayed in any one place since I was 12 years old.

I desperately needed people who cared about me and to look after me through authentic relationships. I could never have told you that because I didn't know. However, I could sense it when people feared me or rejected me. I was just a child, but even as I grew into a young adult, I still struggled to articulate this inability to deal with feeling rejected. When you don't have parents, who respond to your needs, especially in the early years of life, you do not develop the ability to understand what you need to feel safe, secure, and nurtured. My default was always to push people away; you could not trust people because they would be sure to hurt you in some way.

The officers that were smiley and friendly seemed to get underneath this front I was putting on. They asked me if I was, ok? I just nodded.

Nonverbal cues are incredibly powerful when you are dealing with a child like me. I was clearly quite scared, but at the same time, I had to be tough. I didn't know how else to be anyway. They were obviously only being nice because they wanted something from me was my perception. They were just like all the other professionals I had met. Scumbags that could not be trusted. SCREWS! I was introduced to my personal officer (PO). I wasn't rude or aggressive towards her. I didn't really talk back. Looking back, it was how she presented herself and how she spoke to me that broke down these barriers. Treating me with respect and empathising with my situation. Doing so by getting on my level, demonstrating respect and humanity which are elements identified as 'good prison practice' in line with trauma-informed care (see Auty et al., 2022).

She showed me where to do my washing and explained the canteen, phone, and food orders. She showed me where the recreation room was, so I went to sit down. An older woman came over and asked if I was ok. I probably still looked terrified, not that I ever would have admitted it! The woman prisoners on the wing were all outraged that this 15-year-old was in prison in the first place. I wasn't the first, but it didn't happen very often at all. My PO continued to be kind to me, always offering support and asking if I needed anything. I still see her around today she always tells me that she thought I would do well one day and that she is proud of me and what I have achieved. All of which is genuine and when you have had a childhood like mine, knowing this is the superpower. Despite struggling to trust people when I was a child, she always seemed warm, and we never really had a problem, even when I was being challenging. She didn't put her hands on me once because she deescalated situations through relationship-based practice. This was a big change from where I had come from at home, in the children's home and secure. She recently contacted me to ask if I could go and speak to a female prisoner who wants to get involved in work with young people. The careers person at the prison had told her she had no chance with her record, just like I was told. Walking through the female wing I lived on was like walking down memory lane, but it just shows how far I have come and developed as a person. Giving back to the community and helping children who have similar experiences to me is all I have ever wanted to do. To be in this position is not far from a miracle.

When I was in prison, a rule, due to my age, was that I wasn't allowed in the other prisoner's cells and especially not the dorm which had around 10 women prisoners living in it. Of course, I didn't listen, and I was in the dorm all the time. There was a TV in there and a couch.

I didn't have a TV in my cell, and because I wouldn't get up in the mornings, I wasn't allowed one. I remember one Christmas in my cell I was 16. I'd been released, and two months later, I was back on a nine-month prison sentence. This time there was another person or 'young offender' as they called us in there too. She was 17 or 18. To get a TV in our cell for Christmas, we had to get up and do our jobs for a period of a month. I couldn't get out of bed, and they were trying to pay me £15 per month to clean the top landing and bathrooms. I was up to the early hours most nights unable to sleep, but the other person would get up. They moved her cell so she could have the privilege of having the TV over the festive period, and I had to stay in my cell on my own with no TV. Now, if we were taking a trauma-informed approach, would that have happened? I was 16, and I had spent more time inside than outside over the previous three years. I never had stability. I couldn't sleep because I was hypervigilant, and my mind didn't stop sometimes. I'd bash my head on the bars just to stop it from hurting so much. Is it really a good idea to leave a traumatised child in a cell all alone? (Perry, 2007). Some of the older women gave me some weed, so I had something to smoke. This also helped me stop thinking about the pain of life too.

Another time, I was drug tested and I came back positive for cocaine. I remember the officers going mad because they thought someone had given it to me. I was on a wing with about 20–25 other women. My PO told me she needed to talk to me and took me into the office. She didn't tell me off or have a go at me which is just as well because there is a good chance I would not have responded well. She told me that she was worried that I was taking class A drugs. There was another woman, who was in prison with me; let's call her Vicki. Vicki went to the screws and said that there was no way I had taken cocaine, and it was a false positive. She held some weight in what she was saying in the prison and because the screws knew that they believed her. It was indeed a false positive, so I didn't lose my privileges.

I remember this one officer Mary; I would always mess around at bang up, and instead of trying to restrain me and force me into a cell, she used banter to try to get me into my cell. By this point, we had established a relationship. Mary was ok. She was always straight, firm but fair. She was witty with a strong East London accent and used humour to start to build a relationship with me. At no point did I ever feel like she was judging me, even when I returned on a new set of charges just a few months after being released. I still see Mary around; she now works in the reception area of the police station. When I am attending with the young people I now work with, we always have a chat. She is great with young people, and we often laugh about old stories. Once I started the role I am in now, I started to attend the police station regularly with young people. She would often say I needed to be given a promotion so I could have more influence; she'd say 'These young people need examples like you.' Even now, she doesn't hesitate to call through when the police are leaving young people waiting for ages unnecessarily.

Because the wing was small and we were in a mixed prison, although the women's wing was of course separate, the boys Young Offenders Institution (YOI) wing was opposite the female wing. My brother was in the YOI wing on a much longer sentence. When I came into prison, the senior officer on the YOI arranged for me to have two weekly visits with my brother for 30 minutes each time. He recognised that we had both come from difficult backgrounds, and although we still saw each other on and off, we had become separated through the care system and family trauma. Although this is not usual for most prisons, I think it is important to recognise that the prison officer in question demonstrated that he had compassion and empathy for our situation. The same can be done for facilitating other visits recognising that relationships are key for anyone who is wanting to transition away from a life that involved police, courts, and prison.

I remember a schoolteacher from my secure homecoming to teach me at the prison. The first time I went to prison, I was in year 10, imagine. My PO knew what this teacher was about. I didn't realise that she was listening at the door as he was just reminding me that I was a worthless piece of shit that would never achieve anything. He didn't come back again. I didn't realise for some time that she had heard that conversation and observed how I was after. She raised what had happened, and even when I was released and returned to the alternative education establishment, he was not allowed to teach me. My PO clearly cared and recognised that this behaviour was only causing me further trauma. That this was an abuse of power so she did what a good prison officer should do and acted. It was important that she acted because it made my prison experience better. I started to develop some trust in her. No one did stuff like that for me, that guy had slammed me on the floor and shoved me in a cell over and over. He abused his power and used manipulation to make me believe it was all my fault because of how I reacted to him or his situations.

I didn't get on with all the officers. Some struggled that I behaved at times like an angry 15-year-old, and they were not equipped to deal with me challenging them. They were aware that I was a child and could not be treated the same as an adult, but they just didn't understand what that meant within child first principles. We need to better understand how to embed child-first principles into custody for children (Case & Haines, 2021). Children in custody are still children and the environment can stimulate their anxieties because prison can be a dangerous and stressful situation. Prison officers working with this group need to understand the science behind complex trauma and childhood adversity and how this can negatively impact on both physiological and neurological development (Shonkoff et al., 2012).

I couldn't write this chapter without mentioning another officer. I met him briefly in prison, and he worked on the wing with my brother. After I had my son, I knew I needed a hobby; sport has always been important to me and that's when I started Brazilian Jiu-jitsu and boxing. This officer was a boxing coach in the gym I attended. I wanted to fight, and he could see I trained hard. I showed up and put the work in. He started giving me 1–1 sessions for free. He seemed to like training anyone who wanted to fight, but especially those who came from difficult backgrounds. If we put in the work, he was happy to give us some time and knowledge.

Although I was not in prison at the time, I told him about wanting to get into this line of work with children who like me were locked up and did not have anyone they could trust. He could see the barriers I had, and he felt the injustice. I just remember him always telling me I could do whatever I wanted – to keep pushing in the same way I pushed in the gym. 'There is no I can't – it's always you can, it's all in your mind and you can achieve it' he would say to inspire me. I was always driven and ambitious, and having someone in your ear telling you *can* especially when you know they genuinely mean it and believe in you makes you push that bit harder. Martial arts can be a powerful tool to help people recover from trauma, learn how to understand discipline, manage our emotions under intense pressure, breathe properly during challenging situations, and build resilience. Now, this wasn't in prison, but he is a prison officer – imagine if you as officers were inspiring prisoners like this on the inside, what a difference that would make.

My Advice from the Inside

While my prison experience was between the ages of 15–18 and you may be working with people older, I think it's important to try to understand what happened before prison. What happened to this person that led to them being in prison? Understanding the impact of childhood trauma, especially for those with a care experience who were in custody as children, opens a space for compassion and empathy-based conversations. Ford et al. (2019) found that those of us that entered custody as children had been exposed to higher levels of adverse childhood experience. The same study found the prison population also had higher levels of childhood adversity than the general population. Prisoners that grow up in contact with the justice system need to be understood from a position of poverty, inequality, racism, trauma, and addiction. We make poor choices that impact others and create victims, this is true. However, we have often been a victim of social justice with no authority to protect us. Prison officers can influence our behaviours, but it starts with believing in who we are as people so we can believe in ourselves.

No intervention, worksheet, or planned piece of work made a difference in my life; it was people. If I was a prison officer, I would be asking myself questions like, how do I help this person strengthen relationships? What are their challenges inside and outside? Gang crime? Addiction? Returning to traumatic experiences? Homelessness? Before you can understand any of that, you first have to have a relationship, which takes time, and do the extra things that other people don't. It's not about breaking your back, but if can you help, just do it. Be kind, be genuine and offer a hand of support when they need it. I have found that participation and coproduction support young people to recognise and harness the skills they have developed. As a prison officer, ask yourself how you're harnessing the skills of prisoners.

I was a child. I just needed stability and people who were authentic, and relationship focussed. I was years away from talking about my struggles because my relational needs weren't met by my family, or many of the professionals that worked with me. When I look back, it's the prisoners and the two officers; I mentioned that illustrated that not everyone is a bad person or bad practitioner. This is the influence that a Good Prison Officer can have. The seed was planted; it just needed to be replanted and watered repeatedly. This is the value of creating a recovery-orientated prison. It is more than just the prison officers; it is the leaders. It is Her Majesties Prison and Probation Service (HMPPS) and the Ministry of Justice (MOJ) making sure the training is right and prison officers are treated right so they can take care of us. Recovering from trauma is not an easy task; it takes time. Recovery processes must start somewhere. Usually, with that one person who makes a difference. That difference could and should be you as *The Good Prison Officer.*

References

Auty, K. M., Liebling, A., Schliehe, A., & Crewe, B. (2022). What is trauma-informed practice? Towards operationalisation of the concept in two prisons for women. *Criminology & Criminal Justice*, 17488958221094980.

Case, S., & Haines, K. (2021). Abolishing youth justice systems: children first, offenders nowhere. *Youth Justice*, 21(1), 3–17.

Brierley, A. (2021). *Connecting with young people in trouble: Risk, relationships and lived experience*. Waterside Press.

Cicchetti, D., Rogosch, F. A., & Toth, S. L. (2006). Fostering secure attachment in infants in maltreating families through preventive interventions. *Development and Psychopathology*, 18(3), 623–649.

Corrigan, F. M., Fisher, J. J., & Nutt, D. J. (2011). Autonomic dysregulation and the window of tolerance model of the effects of complex emotional trauma. *Journal of Psychopharmacology*, 25(1), 17–25.

Creaney, S. (2020). Children's voices—are we listening? Progressing peer mentoring in the youth justice system. *Child Care in Practice*, 26(1), 22–37.

Creaney, S., & Case, S. (2020). Promoting social inclusion: Participatory rights alternatives to risk discourses in youth justice. *Handbook of Social Inclusion: Research and Practices in Health and Social Sciences*, 1–20.

Felitti, V. J., Anda, R. F., Nordenberg, D., Williamson, D. F., Spitz, A. M., Edwards, V., & Marks, J. S. (1998). Relationship of childhood abuse and household dysfunction to many of the leading causes of death in adults: The Adverse Childhood Experiences (ACE) Study. *American Journal of Preventive Medicine*, 14(4), 245–258.

Fitzpatrick, C., Hunter, K., Shaw, J., & Staines, J. (2022). *Disrupting the routes between care and custody for girls and women*. Lancaster University & The Nuffield Foundation.

Ford, K., Barton, E., Newbury, A., Hughes, K., Bezeczky, Z., Roderick, J., & Bellis, M. (2019). Understanding the prevalence of adverse childhood experiences (ACEs) in a male offender population in Wales: The prisoner ACE survey.

France, A., & Homel, R. (2006). Societal access routes and developmental pathways: Putting social structure and young people's voice into the analysis of pathways into and out of crime. *Australian & New Zealand Journal of Criminology*, 39(3), 295–309.

Gray, P., Smithson, H., & Jump, D. (2021). *Serious youth violence and its relationship with adverse childhood experiences*.

Hambrick, E. P., Brawner, T. W., & Perry, B. D. (2019a). Timing of early-life stress and the development of brain-related capacities. *Frontiers in Behavioral Neuroscience*, 183.

Hambrick, E. P., Brawner, T. W., Perry, B. D., Brandt, K., Hofmeister, C., & Collins, J. O. (2019b). Beyond the ACE score: Examining relationships between timing of developmental adversity, relational health and developmental outcomes in children. Archives of Psychiatric Nursing, 33(3), 238–247.

Laming, H. (2016). *In care, out of trouble: How the life chances of children in care can be transformed by protecting them from unnecessary involvement in the criminal justice system*. Prison Reform Trust.

Perry, B. D. (2007). Stress, trauma and post-traumatic stress disorders in children. *The Child Trauma Academy*, 17, 42–57.

Perry, B. D., & Szalavitz, M. (2017). *The boy who was raised as a dog: And other stories from a child psychiatrist's notebook–What traumatized children can teach us about loss, love, and healing.* Hachette.

Shonkoff, J. P., Garner, A. S., Siegel, B. S., Dobbins, M. I., Earls, M. F., & Wood, D. L. (2012). The lifelong effects of early childhood adversity and toxic stress. *Pediatrics, 129*(1), e232–e246.

Smithson, H., & Jones, A. (2021). Co-creating youth justice practice with young people: Tackling power dynamics and enabling transformative action. *Children & Society, 35*(3), 348–362.

Van der Kolk, B. (2014). *The body keeps the score: Mind, brain and body in the transformation of trauma.* Penguin.

6 From Adversity to University

Daniel Whyte, Prison Number - A3756AW

Who Am I?

This is one of many pieces of work which I have produced. However, I believe that this will be the most important, to date, of my body of work. I state this before telling you who I am simply because I feel that my experiences and subsequently lived experience (LE) knowledge, which will form the content of this chapter, is so much more significant than the person writing it. I wanted to set the tone and context of my words before me.

My name is Daniel Whyte. Dan in my professional and academic circles – which is important to note as it is a deliberate distinction/separation I make for several reasons. I hope this will become clear as you read on. I am the co-founder and co-director of a social enterprise called 'Doing What Really Matters' or DWRM CIC. I have a business partner who is the other co-founder and co-director named Ruth McFarlane. We are both academics (impostor syndrome sits with me daily) and have extensive knowledge of the criminal justice system, albeit from very different vantage points. We are completely aligned in our reasons for doing what we do. The passion we have for this work and, of course, our end goals are borne of one mind.

DWRM is a company with three main divisions which feed directly into one another and create, we hope, a clear pathway with a start and a finish, and everything in between for all who make use of our service provision. This was established and incorporated as a social enterprise, as opposed to a limited company for one reason; it aligned with our social missions, one of which is to provide and foster a clear, strong pathway to rehabilitation through experience-led consultancy, advocacy and administration, facilitating Further and Higher Education in prison. For us to truly work towards and be successful in this mission, the focus can never be about profit! I do not hug trees and am no saint.

DOI: 10.4324/9781003349747-6

I, like most of us like the idea of being comfortable and having nice things. However, I need to do something that matters more and 'not-for-profit' helps keep me focused on what I set out to accomplish. Our second social mission is, 'to provide specialist "Through the Gate" services to allow released students [and those already in the community] to realise academic success, create a career-driven pathway and achieve a pro-social lifestyle.' This second mission statement goes to what I mentioned above, 'a clear pathway with a start and a finish.'

We set up this company first to significantly increase (and improve) the provision of higher and further education for people in prison. Many have had negative experiences in the education system before going to prison, and this often masks an intellectual ability and a voice which needs to be heard. A lack of opportunity to pursue university-level education means that people are denied access to professional roles where they can engage in policy-making, have an influence on the very systems that contributed to their disadvantage, and have the freedom of choice to study the subjects that interest them and with the institutions of their choice. Based on an understanding of education within the prison estate, both Ruth and I have been aware that this is a situation which, up to this point, has been dire, broken, and in serious need of a model that works.

Secondly, as there is currently very limited support for people on release, this tends to mean students are unable to complete their course due to the difficulties of transitioning from a student in prison to one in the community or getting to the point where they are able to sit the required exams. Such students become disillusioned and often lost in terms of continuing with their education. We bridge that gap by providing post-release support to enable students to attend university campuses to complete their degree and or any other course they may be studying. We have a whole menu of services which provide skills training in the areas someone leaving prison or already in the community will need to get themselves ready for or into any form of Education Training and Employment (ETE) which suits them. We have a career-focused provision, devised with the knowledge and an understanding that there is a need for everything from digital literacy skills, and readiness to work to advocacy on behalf of the individual to secure places at educational institutions. We complement this work by assigning everyone with a LE mentor who will support them in whatever ways best suit them and help them apply the training we offer to their own situation and circumstances.

Thirdly, we want to enable people in prison or those in the community with convictions, recent or otherwise, to have a voice. We know that the voice of LE can be extremely powerful and a lot of people can, and want to, contribute both while they are serving and post sentence to the running of prisons, the policies, planning, and advocating for improvements and initiatives which will positively affect them. We have designed and run a series of workshops with people in prison, staff, and prisoners which are delivered by people with LE. We are setting a standard which attributes the value of that LE by paying our facilitators for their time and according to their contributions, much the same as any other sector or employment. We are building a platform for our speakers and facilitators so they can be booked and offered work by anyone who sees and wants to utilise, the value of their LE voice.

So, what qualifies us to create this model and know what is wrong in order to be the ones to fix it, you might ask? Well, let me give you a little background on my business partner before me. Ruth is a woman who has worked as an educator for over 30 years and has built her knowledge base working with many different cohorts of students of all ages. She has delivered higher education in prison, as the senior manager of the previous main provider for several years and has and does teach/lecture in universities. These qualifications, skills, and experience enable her to understand provision on a macro scale which is exactly what is needed for what we do.

I am someone who has had extensive experience with the criminal justice system serving a long prison sentence. During this time, I learned all there was to know about prison and not just how to survive prison. I sought to understand the processes which frame the running of prisons and the cultures which determine the ways the processes are interpreted. Learning about the people who live and work within this estate, who they were and are, and why they were and are there. But most significantly, I needed understanding, and to get to know myself. So, at this point, I want to provide you with an overview. With some relevant detail of my past so that you can understand the seismic shifts in my thinking, attitudes, behaviour, and identity. Knowing my starting point will aid in that understanding. It will also give you context as to what I carried around with me and, therefore, how my interactions with members of the prison staff both negatively and positively impacted my journey.

I was born into a one-parent inner-city family. The youngest of all my siblings and the last to get noticed. In a family that did not have much and would be considered relatively poor in any setting. My mother worked three jobs which only amounted to covering the basics. Going on the 'roads' or on the streets with the sole purpose of making money illegally – was something I saw my older brothers and friends from the local area having to do as a necessity for food and clothing. The first time I had a new [and decent] pair of trainers as a teenager was when my brother bought them for me. I was repeatedly told by my mother that she could not afford them. This was the way in which I was introduced to life, seeing other kids my age able to be kids and having all the things one would expect to be provided. Having to grow up before time.

School was a state school education. Classrooms with pupil sizes at an average of 30–35, and no individual attention from teachers regardless of ability and or needs. It was drummed into me by my older siblings that we, as a family, all needed to bring money in to help our mother keep the house and bills in check. My father was present at home up until I reached the age of 3 years old. He left after trying to kill my mother. In those days, domestic abuse and partner violence was treated differently by the criminal justice system, and for reasons which remain unclear, he was never prosecuted. In fact, he then went onto fight my mother for custody of us and was awarded shared custody – weekends and holidays! This meant that the abuse he directed at my mother was then conferred onto us, the children. Violence: physical, psychological, and emotional abuse became the norm. Being exposed to such violence from a young age and for sustained periods of time – are what I have now come to know as Multiple Adverse Childhood Experiences (MACEs) (Anda et al., 2014) – led to my siblings and myself becoming desensitised to violence. I began my teenage years being a violent child, seeing earning money illegally as work, a job, and most notably, school as an unhappy waste of time.

The ways in which I earned money became more violent, by any means necessary, and by the age of 15, I was serving my first sentence for a 'bit of work' (Robbery). Being sentenced to 5 ½ years for an offence committed when I was 15 years old, as a first conviction, went a long way to confirm what I had been told by my older siblings and peers. We are born with a disadvantage; being poor and black means that we do not get the same opportunities as other people. This is the thinking that pervaded my young mind. This thinking gave me the 'permission' to commit crimes and justify my actions which, ultimately, led to an escalation in the seriousness of offences, all in the name of trying to get what, I saw as, everyone else having. I had, unknowingly, developed an abject irrational fear of being poor as I made it into adult-hood and thought that I had to do whatever it takes not to be poor.

I was released from that first sentence with a newfound rugby career and a life that I never thought I would have and spent most of the time expecting it to be taken from me. When I suffered a career-ending injury, my expectations were confirmed. Although this was just an unfortunate accident, at the time, I felt it as more injustice and irrationally blamed the way the world was, as I had experienced it, as the reason. By this time now, I was a young man 20 years old. I lived with my partner and had to provide although, now I had no income. I was back on the 'roads' in no time at all. However, now I had lost all hope. I took to illegal earnings with earnestness and started to commit robberies as it was a way of making money that I had a natural affinity for and was able to use an unbalanced moral justification, reasoning that it was an honourable form of crime. In terms of the 'streets' and what was acceptable, robbery was right up there. There was no deceit, creeping around people's homes in the middle of the night like burglars or siphoning off people's accounts like fraudsters.

Thinking and behaviour of this sort resulted in a conviction for robbery and joint enterprise. In 2002 I received a life sentence with a 20-year minimum tariff. Twenty-three years old and my life felt as though it was over. I had nowhere left to plummet too; this was rock bottom. Lost and imprisoned with no direction, purpose, or hope, I was teetering on edge. During the induction phase of entering a long-term prison, I was made aware that all prisoners had to complete an educational assessment which, to me, felt punitive as I had negative memories of school and learning. I resisted at first, believing that I would be opening myself up to something I did not want to be exposed to once again – and feeling as though studying in any form seemed like a waste of time that I would not be putting myself through without good reason.

My Prison Experience

Trying to find my feet with the 20-year sentence I had just been handed and got to grips with all things high security was at the forefront of my thinking. 'Doing' education did not even feature. So, it caught me by surprise when I was called to the education department of the high-security prison. Only to be told I had to complete an education diagnostic/assessment of my numeracy and literacy levels to have an Independent Learner Plan (ILP) opened for me. Whilst in the process of refusing any education, the prison officer who was on education that day asked to have a word with me. First positive impact. He then proceeded to give me a few 'home truths,' starting with,

> 'Listen Dan (yes, he called me by my first name, something I found surprising considering this was one of the high security dispersal prisons), you will be doing this sentence for a long time which is going to mean keeping busy all that time. What are you going to do for the next 17 or so years? Eyeroll. I know that I am already

sounding like I am preaching to you so I will stop right here. But let me give you one piece of advice that you can take or leave…'

and what he said next struck a chord with me and became my roadmap through the rest of my sentence. '…if you exercise your body and exercise your mind, you will get through anything!'

Those in authority whose job it was to care for and manage the people locked up on their wings/units were a varied group of staff, both good and bad, which is a consistent feature throughout this collection of chapters. In my case, I experienced the 'bad' prison officers in a slightly different way to most as those who, in the main, were considered 'decent screws' were the ones I had the run-ins and negative interactions with. I generally wasn't considered a control problem in the wings as I was more interested in just getting on with this sentence than standing out, causing problems, and getting a name for being anti… well, anything. Therefore, this interaction with a member of the 'other side' was out of the ordinary for me. It was different from all I had encountered to that point. Most ranged from disinterested and ambivalent to passive-aggressive and spiteful, looking for any opportunity to wield their 'power' over us. Although not a control problem, hindsight showed me that I was a difficult person to be around then and didn't talk to 'screws' past, 'can I have or can I go…' those most basic and minimal of interactions. I thought they [prison officers] were all the same, a belief which had been formed during my past experiences with prison staff and proven by my negative attitudes and their responses to it. What I came to realise further into my sentence and study journey, was that the way I behaved, thought, and believed in a lot of instances, shaped the way I was perceived and treated by prison officers. Conversely, though, the way I perceived and treated those same officers was largely shaped by my adverse childhood experiences or early life traumas, which I will go on to talk about in more detail.

'Doing' the sentence was by no means easy. I had a lot of very difficult days and hard times which were a struggle to get through. The person who is writing this now is so far from the person that started the sentence, so much so that if I walked past the old me, I would not recognise him. The only part of that person I still remember is the realisation I had, standing in the middle of a cell one day, maybe two or three days after the 'home truths' conversation, that I had to change my life. At the time, I had no real idea what that meant or how to go about it. By the time I started studying, I was motivated and eager to learn, but I was directionless. Following the completion of the basic literacy and numeracy level 1 and 2s, the first step on my road to academia was obtaining my General Certificate of Secondary Education (GCSEs) of which I successfully completed 5, then 4 A levels and with that under my belt came the realisation that there was more to life than whatever had come before. I started a journey of Higher Education study that took me through an access to Higher Education course, an undergraduate degree, and then a Postgraduate degree. It is funny because I remember thinking at the start of the access course that 'I did not have a clue what I wanted from my studies' – other than a degree – and more importantly, I had no idea what it could do for me. As I encountered the type of problems that life in prison involves, and as I later found, the differing challenges that come from studying – when it clashes with the prison regime and life.

The skills I needed to complete a degree whilst in prison, interestingly, were also the skills I needed to successfully navigate my way through prison life. They started to manifest themselves in me: self-motivation, self-discipline, determination, steadfastness, and in particular instances, sheer doggedness. The thought of not reaching my newfound goal became entwined with my survival instincts and made me more determined, as I put more into my studies, I began to see the benefits as I received my results. I was awarded 'Student of the Year' and in fact, I was the first recipient of this award, and from that point, I can truly say that studying changed my outlook on life. Unfortunately, though, this is where a lot of the most overtly biased interactions with prison officers manifested themselves.

Juxtaposed with the positive internal growth spurts I was having, prison officers started to notice these changes in my behaviour and attitude and proceeded to interact with and want to engage me in conversation. On the surface, these were pleasant, just them wanting to 'get to know me better.' However, when asking about what I was studying, and what I wanted to do with the qualifications I was achieving and working towards, there was a frequency of similar responses like, 'I wish someone would give me the opportunity to study...,' 'you lot are lucky you get to study for free...,' 'prisoners get so much...!' – and we wonder why there is this common misconception out there in wider society when they are perpetuated by voices, who supposedly, know better. Statements like that then feed those sun readers, as we called them in prison, who think and say ignorant nonsense like prisons are holiday camps. Negative impact. However, when it came to wing reports being written, or those occasions which called for an officer to show some compassion, understanding and utilise the relationship building I assumed they had been doing with me, the personal thoughts and feelings behind those earlier statements mentioned earlier, surfaced. Let me give one such example.

I walked back onto my wing after being at the gym on one Tuesday afternoon and was stopped by an officer – who I thought was ok (due to conversations of the sort above). He asked me to come into the office and shut the door behind me. He then proceeded to inform me that he had received a call from a member of my family telling me that my son had been attacked, beaten, and robbed on his way home from school. My son was 12 years old at the time. I was visibly upset, thinking the worst and experiencing a range of emotions – from fear for my son, to uselessness at my inability to protect him, and or do anything substantial at that point. Realising that I didn't have any phone credit on my pin phone to call home, I asked if he would give me a call on the office phone. His response was that he would ask the S.O. (senior officer) but was sure it wouldn't be a problem. He said as soon as he had completed the wing movements (prisoners moving to and from work and other activities), he would call me on the tannoy and give me the call. Understanding this would take a while; I went up to my landing to take a shower and change after the gym. Approximately 45 minutes went by and once I realised, I wasn't being called I went down to the office to ask what was going on.

The officer was sitting behind the desk in the office and as he looked up and saw me. I recognised the expression on his face; he had forgotten. However, the logical next step in that situation would have been to just say something along the lines of, 'sorry I got caught in some other work but will do it now.' Instead, this officer decided to go a different way. Before I had a chance to speak, he said, 'I asked the S.O. and he said no.' I was caught off-guard by that at first and then became angry. I turned on my heels and walked down the corridor and knocked on the S.O.'s door. When I asked why I was not allowed a call, it became instantly obvious that he had no idea what I was talking about. After giving him a quick synopsis of what I had been told about my son, he picked up the phone, asked me for the number, dialled, and then handed me the phone once it started to ring. After I had finished my call and hung up, I thanked the S.O. and then told him that the officer had lied to me using him as an excuse. I left the office on the back of him, saying he would be speaking to the officer in question.

A short time later, I heard my name called over the tannoy and made my way back to the S.O.'s office to be confronted by the officer (the messenger, the liar), another officer, and the S.O. The S.O. said that he had been told a different account by these two officers, supposedly now I had stormed into the office telling them, that my son had been attacked and demanding they give me a call there and then otherwise, 'there would be trouble!' I felt like I had just stepped through a wardrobe into an alternate universe where everything was worse... if that was possible. Dumbfounded at what I was hearing, plus considering the origin of this whole situation being that I had just been given the worst news as a father in prison, that my son was in the hospital and the police were waiting to speak to him, etc. And I was NOT there or able to rush to be by my son's side. Now I was being faced with dumb and dumber concocting an even Dumberer story for what seemed like absolutely no reason that I could see. My reply... 'they are lying!' and then proceeded to recount the situation as it had happened. But before the S.O. could respond, the first officer (dumb) jumped back in and stated the line which stayed with me to this day and almost threw me off-course entirely. 'Whyte, is studying a psychology degree and thinks he is smarter than everyone else and is using his intelligence to manipulate this situation sir!'

The S.O. then turned to the officer and stated, if you are sure, then you must place Mr Whyte on report. Which he did. I left that office the most confused, angry, and disillusioned, I think, I had ever been at the vindictiveness of people in positions of authority and power. At this point, it is important to note that I was a prisoner who held two of the most trusted jobs within that establishment and was also given a lot of freedom of movement – which was the only reason I was able to maintain my degree study alongside the positions I held. They enabled me to go up to the education department whenever I needed to and jump on any spare computer that was available to do and complete study work. This set-up was contingent on me keeping warning, Incentive and Earned Privileges (IEP) and adjudication free. It was now all in jeopardy based on a lie! He followed through with the adjudication, and therefore, the next day, I was in front of the governor while dealing with the anxiety of not knowing how my son was recovering. The usual stresses of prison life and now the unpredictability of this situation.

I presented my case to the governor, who, to his credit, got it straight away but was then bound by process and stated that he needed to hear from the officer who placed me on the report because I was contesting his account, and in fact levelling a serious accusation of my own. Just my luck, the reporting officer was now off for 10 days, and therefore, the adjudication had to be adjourned until his return. This meant that in effect I was now serving a punishment as I would be suspended from my jobs and my freedom of movement was also taken away. This resulted in not being able to get to the education department amongst other things, and as sod's law goes, I had an assignment due. I had no means of being able to type it up and submit it on time. Negative impact. That period was extremely stressful, disheartening, and created feelings of distrust, dislike, and trauma. The effects of which stayed with me for a long time, or more accurately, never left me. Being a person with a significant amount of resilience, determination, and single-minded focus, I was able to rely on those resources to keep me on track and channel the negative energy as fuel.

Three weeks went by with no resolution, no word from the governor and I wasn't called back for the adjudication. I put in applications and complaint forms and asked members of staff to call the segregation unit to try and find out what was going on with my 'nicking.' After missing yet another deadline, and the subsequent extension deadline for my latest degree assignment, I had had enough. The build-up of stress, worry, and tension brought me to breaking point – or the point of blowing my top. It felt torturous. I was a prisoner that worked hard, maintained a high standard of behaviour, and went out of my way to help my peers, and yet, here I was being treated like I had committed a fresh offence and was, as a result of the adjudication process, being punished for needing a call to speak to my son who had been rendered a victim by whatever person out there had singled him out.

I slipped off the wing at the next movement time and went to the governor's suite; being a regular there due to the work and relationships I had built up with the Senior Management Team (SMT), no one questioned my presence as I waited between gates to be let through. I knocked on the open door of the Head of Residence's office and walked in. He took one look at the expression on my face and said, 'sit down and tell me what is going on.' I did. And once I was finished, he picked up the phone and spoke to someone – who was, by the one side of the conversation I could hear, located in the segregation unit. He turned to me and said, 'I am not sure why you haven't been informed or restored to your status but, the nicking has been thrown out. I will call your wing Custodial Manager and make sure you have been put back on work etc.' Relief, anger, and exasperation flooded through me in equal measure. I started to ask a million questions which I had bubbled forth, felt suddenly exhausted, and settled on just one, 'is no one going to reprimand this officer for what he has done?!' His reply typified all that is wrong with the prison service; 'Dan, you know how it is, just be thankful it is sorted now, and you haven't lost anything.'

Whilst still in prison, I was offered places on projects and to work with academics while they completed prison-related research. This is also the time when I was introduced to Convict Criminology, which is a conceptual component of criminology formed by a group of ex-convict and non-convict academics that share similar philosophies and actively seek to reform. This is done by empowering the voices of those with LE of prison and the sentences served within them, by providing a platform and promoting the work of this new breed of academics. As someone who wanted to be heard and was eager to facilitate change within our criminal justice system, I felt compelled to immerse myself in convict criminology. As this account brings us to date, I can say with certainty that I am now part of a community which has been accepting of the person I was, an uneducated, directionless criminal, and embraces the person I am now, a convict criminologist, PhD student, and company director.

There were multiple incidences like those I have recounted above. However, I have highlighted these as they hopefully provide a slightly different vantage point for what 'good' and 'bad' officers look like to someone who is doing everything expected of them as a prisoner, and more. As a person able to cope with, and overcome the negative impacts of vindictive officers, while at the same time being left scarred by them, I offer these examples for the benefit of those who would be less able to manage these damaging interactions. In the hope that those reading this will get a glimpse of the ways in which their [prison officers] behaviours can determine the course of the prisoners in their care's futures.

My Advice from the Inside

As a serving prisoner turned academic, who used higher education to transform my own life, identity, attitudes, and beliefs to create lasting pro-social bonds, and 'shake off' or at least mitigate the stigma and gain acceptance in society, I could not, as a free man now, separate myself from the people I shared these issues and experiences with. At the point of self-examination, I came to understand that there had to be reasons for my early negative behaviours and the changes which my educational journey helped shape. I was born of an amazing mother who instilled values, morals, and principles in us [my siblings and I] all, granted I had a horribly violent and inadequate father. Yet here I was, a man with a violent past now of my own, but with a newfound sense of morality and principle. How did the negatives of my upbringing override the positive influences in the first place? And how did they reduce my ability to avoid the negative outcomes of my subsequent behaviours of which I am still experiencing the effects? These questions led me to research which revealed firstly that Adverse Childhood Experiences (ACEs) indicators were present in my life, which then led to a more in–depth search for evidence to support – or otherwise – the hypotheses which began to form cognitively within me.

Now, here today, I find myself in a unique position. After having attained the knowledge and understanding first to be self-informed and be able to understand my own life and the tensions created as it buffets up against a society I am once again a part of. I seek to use it alongside my LE, as I do in the role of visiting lecturer and researcher, with anyone who could potentially benefit from it. Please bear with me here as to present my advice from the inside; I need to make the links between these tensions explicit. So, my advice starts here, this prison system is, in my view, irreparably damaged and as such some, most will slip through the rehabilitation net cast out by the prison service. For one reason or another, the processes put in place to fulfil the rehabilitative strand of a prison sentence will be wasted and lost on a large percentage of those who are made to serve time. Indeed, Liebling and Maruna (2005) made an observation that the effectiveness of education and well-designed interventions may well be undermined by the harsh condition of being incarcerated. Therefore, I subscribe to the concept of self-change. This is a process that every prisoner can use as a route to desistence. And will ensure that all who want to change can do so without waiting for or relying on the prison service's provisions to do it for them.

Writers such as Vaughan (2007), states that the role of the individual is significant, and there is a personal agency needed to 'power' a move to and maintain desistance. Maruna (2001) also highlighted the importance of the individual's role and personal agency in desistance, reinforcing the views of Vaughan (2007). Underlying this shift to a pro-social identity is the re-conceptualisation of the self, which is achieved through reconstructing one's internalised life narrative (Maruna & Copes, 2005). Focusing on this argument takes us back a step and gives merit to the individual, which helps build a picture, at least in the setting of incarceration, whereby control is in the hands of the individual to decide to move towards desistance at any point of incarceration. This is the self-change process. Relative to this, Maruna (2001; see also Maruna & Copes, 2005) found that many people in prison assumed generative roles, using their past experiences to help others. Importantly, they attributed self-change to personal agency and expressed how much more meaningful their 'new' lives were.

Self-change is exactly that commanded and executed by the self. Uggen et al. (2004) highlight that the prisoners' commitment to pro-social [attitudes], and hence a law-abiding or conforming sense of self is undermined by the stigma of a criminal conviction which awaits them on the outside. Put simply, it is hard enough for people in prison to change their attitudes and beliefs without the added pressures, perceived or real, of non-acceptance once back in society. The implications for those who have served custodial sentences appear to be more severe, as the enduring stigma of a custodial sentence imposes restrictions on work opportunities, housing choices, and a myriad of other social relationships, perpetuating the isolation prisoners feel whilst incarcerated (Aresti et al., 2010).

Prison officers need to be aware of the internalised struggles we all face(d) as prisoners daily. These, as stated earlier, are invisible and complex as they create tensions within the individual as they try to navigate their way through old behaviours and habits, relationships with their peers who, in some cases, hold them back from change, intentionally or otherwise. Adverse childhood experiences, which, in most cases, have a stranglehold on their negative personality traits create a kind of 'criminogenic and or antisocial fog' which makes it hard to imagine a prosocial future self. The reason for this attempt to explain this from a unique inside perspective is because when you make throw-away comments and allow your own negative views, frustrations, and misuse of power to creep into your professional life, you have no idea of the impacts you will have on prisoners' personal battles with his or herself.

For those of you who are genuinely in the job for the right reasons and have well-intended motivations for turning up at work every day, I am sure this chapter will penetrate deep within. Compassion for your fellow man is something we all aspire to have and exude, so is your fellow man less than your equal because he or she has temporarily had their liberty removed? Secondly, were you put on this earth to judge your fellow man? When we take up roles do we care for the vulnerable and excluded, the answer should never be, yes. However, if, as it should be your answer is no, then consider this; people go to prison for a wide range of reasons, from making a mistake to being stuck in a cycle of offending; this we know. What you don't know is what sits behind that mistake, or what led to the path of offending and what keeps an individual stuck on it. Even when you ask said individuals why, they can only tell you what they can articulate which is usually a mish mash of inaccurate opinions from people not qualified to make those assessments. Sometimes, even professionals do not bother to go beyond the surface and make generalised and incomplete diagnoses. Point is, there is always so much more to any one story than you can or will be aware of. Therefore, if you go to work with an attitude which is something like this, 'I do not know how these individuals got to be in my charge, but I am not going to be the one to mitigate that damage and trauma they may have suffered. I am going to be part of the cycle of change!' Then, the impact you make will never be a negative one. You make either no impact or you impact for good. Either way, you will do no further damage.

It is the little things, be their comments, acts of kindness, or just ensuring your job is done to the best of your ability, that generally have the biggest positive impact on people in prison. This is because we know that your days are full of one job or another. If a prisoner you know is studying, for example, and comes to the office to ask for something seemingly insignificant like paper, go out of your way to help. This is because the people who positively inform the experience of self-change are the ones who are remembered and help create the most lasting impacts. If a prisoner says that he will leave the prison you are standing in and become the director of a company that will positively change a part of the prison system, don't laugh, and make a silly throwaway comment thinking that is impossible – even if you think it is! Help, encourage and show interest. These are the little things that make the most impact.

How do I know, well I am that company director, and I was that prisoner!

References

Anda, R. F., Larkin, H., & Felitti, V. J. (2014). Social work and adverse childhood experiences research: Implications for practice and health policy. *Social Work in Public Health, 29*(1), 1–16.

Aresti, A., Eatough, V., & Brooks-Gordon, B. (2010). Doing time after time: An interpretative phenomenological analysis of reformed ex-prisoners' experiences of self-change, identity and career opportunities [Article]. *Psychology, Crime & Law, 16*(3), 169–190. https://doi.org/10.1080/10683160802516273.

Liebling, A., & Maruna, S. (2005). *The effects of imprisonment*. Willan.

Maruna, S. (2001). *Making good* (p. 86). American Psychological Association.

Maruna, S., & Copes, H. (2005). What have we learned from five decades of neutralization research? *Crime and Justice, 32*, 221–320.

Uggen, C., Manza, J., & Behrens, A. (2004). *After crime and punishment: pathways to offender reintegration*. Willan Publishing.

Vaughan, B. (2007). The provision of policing and the problem of pluralism: Theoretical criminology. London. *England: SAGE Publications, 11*(3), 347–366.

7 We're Only Human

Devon Ferns, Prison Number - 207689

Who Am I?

My name is Devon Ferns. I am a 20-year-old professional currently working with children and young people in a great South Yorkshire city. I am currently working through an apprenticeship as a Youth Support Worker for Rotherham's Early Help Services. Most call me Dev and I grew up in sunny Rotherham. To be more specific, a small area in Rotherham called Kimberworth Park, which is known locally as 'Kimi,' is the stomping ground. I don't want to explain why the area developed this name as I do not want to stigmatise the area any more than it has been over the years. I will leave this interpretation up to your imagination. It is a community that is faced with deprivation and challenges like other areas dealing with the negative consequences of inequality and lack of opportunity. Again, as with most areas such as mine, most of the people support each other in various ways, even though many of them are facing hardship and poverty.

Growing up in this estate did unfortunately mean I experienced childhood poverty which many studies have shown is damaging for the child's mind body and soul, leading to poor health outcomes, into adolescence and beyond (Duncan et al., 2012; Spencer, 2003; Tampubolon, 2015; Wickham et al., 2016). However, I have managed to use these experiences positively in my early career in Children's Services. The first-hand insight into such experiences combined with the knowledge I am developing in my apprenticeship through education enhances my ability to take a trauma-informed approach with the children I work with. What I would describe as an equal and sensitive practice approach to connect with children in trouble with the law (Wright et al., 2016). Being Present and Attuned develops Connections that formulate Trusting (PACT) relationships (Brierley, 2021).

DOI: 10.4324/9781003349747-7

Within my current role as a youth support worker, I am responsible for facilitating a participation group for justice-involved children named CHANCE Group (Rotherham Children's Services Peer Review, 2022; see also Peer Power/YJB, 2021). The approach I take is grounded in Harts Ladder of Participation of ensuring children are empowered to have a voice and influence policy and service strategy in Rotherham's Children's Services (Hart, 2008). Hart developed this model in 1992 as a metaphor to start discussions about how to develop ideas to ensure children are actively involved in decision-making with adults. The group I am currently working with is making music videos, developing training packages for senior management of various services, and engaging other children as role models to take on leadership roles. I encourage them to use the skills and knowledge that they have developed growing up in similar challenging social spaces to benefit others. To share their understanding of service delivery of support services for the benefit of justice-involved youth as experiential peers and help professionals understand how to best work with others in their position (Creaney 2020; Lenkens et al., 2021).

This elevating and participatory approach to improving outcomes for socially disadvantaged children derives from my own personal experiences of the youth justice and care systems. There is some evidence found in recent studies that there are in fact four key mechanisms that evolve between experiential peers and clients or children in a criminal justice setting. These are that experiential peers demonstrate empathy and an unjudgmental approach. Children see experiential peers as credible role models that can demonstrate that such backgrounds can be used to *make good*. Experiential peers provide visual examples that life beyond offending is possible and realistic. The shared experiences can develop a trusting bond because of our shared identities. Lastly, experiential peers focus on recovery as opposed to an expectation that desistance is a linear process (Lenkens, 2022; Maruna, 2001). When it comes to supporting desistance, which is the cessation of offending, the criminal justice system should facilitate more opportunities to 'give back' for those of us that are expected to 'give up' as it can often become a generative process of developing a prosocial identity (McNeill & Maruna, 2007). If we can influence each other's behaviour within communities such as mine in a negative way, surely when we have desisted from offending, we can use these experiences to influence each other in a positive way. Becoming a 'wounded healer' so to speak can develop a generative concern for others which helps us move on from where we have been to where we are going (Maruna & Ramsden, 2004).

Reading the next phase of my chapter, I want to reiterate that I am providing my own personal experience of youth incarceration. That not every child or young person who has had any individual experience will share the same views on all matters. There are limitations as I present my experiences. I understand that other prisoners and prison officers may have an alternative perspective of the very same events. However, it is the view of many of us with lived realities of the justice system that justice organisations will improve in their responses to crime if they include the 'wisdom of those with the lived experience' (Harriott, 2021, p. 78). This is the essence of the growing discipline of narrative criminology which has been argued as a 'useful framework for critical criminology' (Presser & Sandberg, 2015 p.11). We as a group have often been excluded from the conversations about how best to support us to desist from crime, and this approach ensures that there is an avenue for us to positively engage. I hope my contribution to this book helps prison officers understand and support desistance of others like myself caught up in my past circumstances to move forward with hope.

Furthermore, I believe it is important to point out that although the justice system and incentive schemes worked for me personally, the message of my chapter is that not every young person gets the same opportunity due to their 'Presenting behaviour' or in my opinion 'survival skills.' The reason I suggest many children present survival skills is because from my perspective I have found that young people who do not respond well to challenging environments and traumatic interpersonal experiences seem to naturally develop survival skills. This often determines how they communicate and navigate challenging spaces as well as how they perceive and respond to authority and support services. As this book is about prison officer practice and how to be a good prison officer, I will explore this through a personal lens or my experience of both good and bad practice. I will aim to demonstrate how much of an impact prison officers can have on a young person's life when they spend time in Young Offenders Institutions (YOIs) and Secure Training Centre's (STCs).

My Prison Experiences

When growing up, me and my mum didn't really see eye to eye. However, now I'm older, I can see that she had her own challenges and childhood trauma to deal with alongside trying to deal with me and my unique qualities or response to these interpersonal challenges shall we say. This is often described as the intergenerational cycle of trauma. The experiences of trauma not being dealt with by a parent inadvertently and often subconsciously transmit that pain to their off-spring. Studies have found that 'the odds of a child experiencing phys-ical maltreatment were three to five times greater among mothers who had a history of abuse or neglect compared with mothers without such a history, depending on the severity of the mother's experiences' (Jaffee et al., 2013). At times this didn't make it easy for me to be parented because I had no capacity, nor maturity to empathise with mum.

Me and my father didn't have the best relationship either growing up. Therefore, in my teens, like many children from families like mine, I developed a family within my friendship group and peers. I wish I could say I was very smart growing up. However, to be truthful, I was far from academic. Being streetwise was something that I valued because I was quite savvy and felt that I got more respect in the street than in my classroom. Prior to my time in custody, I spent around 90 percent of my time outside with friends. That's where I felt safe for various reasons which was largely because this is where I developed my strongest attachment to relationships. I would describe my attachment style at this stage as disorganised which is a predictor of aggression in childhood (see Lyons-Ruth, 1996. With hindsight, I now feel as though developing those relationships with my peers was helping me to deal with the troubles I was having at home, and maybe subconsciously finding a father figure or role model to look up to because of the absent one at home. Again, I think this was all part of me building my sur-vival skills and developing my own sense of independence which was a word professionals often use. I think we should be teaching children to be interdependent on inclusive communities because children should always have interconnected relationships.

However, when I was in my mid-teens, I found myself in a difficult situation where I was facing a serious charge and a very lengthy custo-dial sentence for a serious crime. As you can imagine, this was a very challenging time for me as a 15-year-old. I was having to deal with the whole justice system, including the processes and legal jargon that I could not understand due to my capacity or language difficulties. Not that I was alone. Research shows this is the case for many other children caught up in the legal system (see Bryan et al., 2015). Adding this, I was tackling my own childhood trauma and family breakdown because of my behaviour. Not long before I was arrested, my mum and dad had separated and my mum had found a new boyfriend who seemed to be the positive influence that could indeed break the cycle. Unfortunately, whilst I was on trial, me and him didn't really build a positive relation-ship and due to one thing or another, we ended up having a physical altercation. The result of this was that my mum dropped me off at court the next day with £6 and a couple of cigs and told me not to come home. At this point, I was very lucky to have Keryn (my YOT worker) who arranged for some family friends to foster me and prevented me from entering the mainstream care system. Although my situation was difficult, this made a difference because the link between the care and justice system is well documented and the outcomes for this group can be one of the poorest (see Fitzpatrick & Williams, 2017). However, I do not want this chapter to be about my childhood trauma. These are just several examples to provide some insight into why I titled this chapter, 'we are only human' after experiencing custody so young.

My experience of custody has certainly played a role in shaping my identity. However, what was it about my experience that empowered me to desist after the experience? After a lot of reflection, there were many things that played a part in this. One significant factor was my interaction with Good Prison Officers. Of this, there is absolutely no doubt. From the minute I arrived at the STC, my thoughts, feelings, and emotions were all over the place. At first, I really struggled to understand how I was going to respond to this extremely scary and uncertain situation. The only information that I had about custody or jail was the stereotypes that either my older mates had told me or the misconceptions that films and movies create. The second, I was escorted out of the transport van I remember my first interaction with a prison officer. Fortunately, this was a positive interaction as he explained who he was, and before taking me for my induction, he asked if I wanted any food or drink and tried to get to know me a little. In comparison with Andi's officer interaction in Brinsford in Chapter 2, this is how to be child first, even in custody.

It cannot be overstated how good this practice was or the value of that first impression. I was over 85 miles away from Kimi the Stomping Ground which was my comfort zone. This immediately demonstrated that the stereotypes of 'screws' was possibly wrong and that some do care. It showed me that he cared about me having a comfortable transition from the community to custody and that created a sense of safety when I needed it most. I wanted to highlight this as even though it's a small interaction, this sense of safety influenced how I conducted myself. I was quiet, observant, and didn't really speak much. It seemed to me that the prison officers' calm and approachable practice meant I was inclined to be polite and considerate. However, that is how I deal with new and uncomfortable situations. In my time in custody, I did also witness a lot of children and young people with traumatic experiences and challenging upbringings fail to manage the transition in the way I did. Some of my peers came in being loud or even not speaking at all.

Many of these children were often described as aggressive, non-compliant, or a risky child. In my observation of my vantage point of being a peer, they're just navigating a challenging and uncomfortable carceral space. The survival skills that they have developed as a response to their individual challenges kick in, and they dysregulate when they feel unsafe or uncertain which is often called 'fight or flight' (Andrews et al., 2019). Anyone that has first-hand experience with youth custody will understand how the very thought of prison for children can fuel these emotions. Therefore, every child responds to stressful situations differently. My understanding of this from my inside perspective of custody is that aggression and risk is often misunderstood, and this can be when prison officers respond inappropriately and disproportionately. When this takes place, it really affects the experience of the child. Although I believe these responses are natural to the general members of the public, prison officers need specific training to manage these situations in a way that is trauma informed. Every child should be entitled to the same opportunities I received, regardless of their response to incarceration as a basic right, because they are still children and should be seen as such (Case & Haines, 2021).

I recall the first three months of my sentence being the hardest time of my life, which of course wasn't extensive, but was certainly intensive. Despite a year of investigations and a 12 weeklong trial, I would say that nothing compares to this change in life, environment, relationships, and isolation. These early months tested me both mentally and physically as I was at my lowest and using my survival skills to keep me going. It turns out that the skills I had developed surviving poverty, inequality, childhood trauma, and violence became highly transferrable to staying safe throughout youth incarceration. Something not quite understood when prison staff want you to change at the precise moment that those skills are required. I will never forget the handful of prison staff that supported me through this time, though. The officers took the time to have a one-to-one conversation with me about me and my emotions and feelings as opposed to my behaviour. Taking the time and being curious enough to ask how I was feeling about being in prison. The officers started to prepare me for the future through motivational interviewing techniques that I now use in practice with justice-involved youth (McMurran, 2009).

From my vantage point of incarceration, this was indeed good practice. My life stopped the minute I was arrested; therefore, I didn't even think about the future, let alone plan for it. I remember that I didn't have much of a relationship with my family. My phone calls were few and far between, and this made me feel like a bit of a lone wolf. I felt isolated with very little support from home and that I had to take this challenging journey alone, and the officers that made a difference were the ones that could recognise that this was the case, without me even saying it. They were attuned to my thoughts and feelings and able to understand what was going on. Incredibly important because teenage boys in prison are discouraged from sharing their thoughts and feelings, so this skill is a foundation for becoming The Good Prison Officer. This reality did make my time in custody a lot harder, and the connection with staff is vital for youth, even for youth like me, we are not always able to articulate this to officers.

After around six months of being in custody, I realised that the prison experience was like a merry-go-round. People just seemed to come and go into the establishment. Both prisoners and prison officers and this was unsettling. It reinforces the sense of isolation and loneliness because your time seems to stand still. Due to the time, I had been in custody at this point; I built several good relationships with stable prison officers on the wing. They became as strong as the relationships with other prisoners, or children as I should say. These handful of staff seem to go above and beyond to make me realise that I do have a future. When having discussions with these officers, they would share relevant information about themselves which made them more relatable, and we developed connections (see Brierley, 2021). By this point, although incarceration seems to delay the maturation and the desistance process for many children in custody, these relationships were building hope (Graham & McNeill, 2017), my sense of citizenship and as a result my ability to develop a positive personal narrative (Bateman & Hazel, 2018).

This demonstrates the power of relationships and that relationships can indeed influence desistance in youth, improve outcomes and as a result reduce crime and recidivism. However, relationship needs to become the foci and receive more attention in 'policy and practice' (Graham & McNeill, 2017, p. 10). The interesting issue here for the youth justice system to consider is that the officers involved in developing my sense of hope and citizenship were often those that stepped slightly out of their protected role and gave me something of themselves, which other justice recipients have also indicated to support the desistance process (Rowe & Soppitt, 2014). At this stage in my sentence, I was exploring how to ensure I stayed out when I got out. I started studying which evidence also suggests can be a catalyst or scaffolding for many already considering a change (Szifris et al., 2018). Prior to this, education was not something I ever prioritised before or during my incarceration. It was the relationships with officers and prison staff that certainly influenced my development of starting to consider new ideas and new experiences. One thing that I never thought I would have done was learning to play an instrument. Around seven months into my sentence, I came across a prison officer teaching another prisoner how to play the guitar. I was initially surprised by the prison officer's commitment to use his own personal unique skills to improve the skills of a prisoner. Andi Brierley's chapter defined this as expert power. I asked the officer if he could teach me which introduced me to a new skill and before I knew it, I was like an incarcerated Jimi Hendrix.

A year into my sentence, my mindset had completely changed. I was now able to see past my release date and where I thought I wanted to be in life beyond walking through the gate. I was able to study for a level three qualification to become a personal trainer and gain both my Maths and English General Certificates of Secondary Education (GCSEs). This would not have been possible if the prison officers and education staff hadn't volunteered to be a part of my course work and let me use them as clients in the gym. To elaborate, I understand that the staff didn't have to give their time after their shift to assist me, which allowed me to complete my course work. This was completely voluntary and made me feel valued in the sense that prison officers cared about me and my future and continued to break down feelings of stigma.

On the other hand, there were a few prison staff who weren't like that and didn't have the passion or time to get to know us as prisoners. My viewpoint or sharing of perspective of prison officers needs to be balanced if we are to improve practice and develop a rehabilitative culture. This balance needs to be nuanced if we are to improve children's experience of prison and enhance procedural justice to create the transformational change I experienced, in others not so lucky (see Fitzalan & Wakeling, 2021). In my opinion, it was these sorts of prison officers that tend to find the job hard. This impacts their staying on the job which indicates there is something inadequate about the training prison officers receive which explains the unsustainable level of turnover in the system (Her Majesties Prison and Probation Service (HMPPS), 2021). My key recommendation therefore is that all officers in the youth estate understand the child first principles. That trauma-informed practice is central to their training, so they respond appropriately and stay in post, get job satisfaction, and understand children and how we respond to trauma.

On a positive note, the guitar-playing prison officer (Gary) really started to empower me and develop my motivation and more importantly hope in others (see McNeill et al., 2012). I will never forget Gary coming onto the wing with his own personal Fender Stratocaster and Kustom amp (Guitar and amp). He handed them both to me. He told me and the other young man he taught to play that we could store these in our cells and use them to practice. I wanted to point this out again, as you don't have to bring your personal belongings inside to develop trust with a young person. However, what that did for me was it showed that Gary was providing us with responsibility. It showed that he had trust and compassion for us as prisoners. Gary being the legend he is was often thinking of additional resources whilst not on shift to aid us in progressing with the music. Things like chords and scales. It was not about the guitar. This behaviour showed me that some prison officers don't just forget about us when they get home but hold us in their minds which is what all children want to feel important. That they have an investment in our futures, alleviating the stigma of the shaming prison experience.

After around 15 months, I had settled into prison life. However, my personal experience of custody helped me focus on the future which I would argue was due to the officers that I had a relational experience with. Now I only had five months left. At this point, I would like to point out that the staff on our wing would often take time to discuss my goals with me. More importantly, we would plan for how I could achieve them. I didn't know at the time, but they were using effective Five-Minute Interventions (FMI) (Kenny & Webster 2015). Not every incarcerated child will want to discuss their release with those they don't have a relationship. Officers like Gary were able to develop trust straight away. Not because of FMIs, but because they were relational and invested in me as a human through presenting themselves as human first, officer second, obtaining referent power and legitimising their authority (Steiner & Wooldredge, 2018). Some of our best discussions were around 'what's the first thing you're going to eat' or 'what's your plans for release day.' I think it's important to understand that even though someone's release day may be months away, it's crucial for them to understand that it is coming as some children struggle to see that far. Talking about the release will give them something to strive for and look forward to. It did for me anyway and as in line with Motivational Interviewing (MI), which evidence suggests 'can lead to improvements on measures of readiness or motivation to change' (McMurran, 2009, p. 95).

It was at this point in my sentence, I unfortunately found out that I had lost my granddad due to cancer. Heart-breaking; and it felt like just another knock in this unforgiving childhood. It is important to emphasis this because there was one prison officer who really supported me through this naturally challenging time. Danni, she was not only discreet about my loss. She also provided me with the means to discuss my thoughts and feelings. This enhanced my ability to regulate my emotions using Socio Emotional Learning (SEL) and that I could manage not only my granddad passing, but how to take stock and deal with stressful situations. I remember she came to get me from the education block and what really surprised me was that she had unblocked my phone so I could ring my family. Again, I know that maybe this isn't possible in every establishment as I was in an STC. However, I just wanted to emphasise how she went above and beyond to make sure I was feeling the best I could and offered me as much support as possible. It was a moment when I just thought 'we're in different places, but in the end, *we're only human.*' I also want to add that due to the way Danni conducted herself in relaying information between me and my dad, I didn't feel like I was being seen as a risk, but rather a person or a child. I think youth custody has some way to go for children to be seen as children all the time, which is disappointing given that is a key tenet of Child First principles adopted by the Youth Justice Board (YJB) is to see *children as children* (Case & Haines, 2021).

Danni made me feel like she wanted to know if I was alright for her own personal reasons rather than just for a risk assessment which is how other prison officers can make you feel. In relation to my progression, it was at this point that me, Joe (the other guitarist), and another young man who had come in, started a band as a group of children in a difficult situation. What was surprising was that some of the officers from other wings would come to listen when they could. But what was inspiring was that the officers supported us to hold a gig in the main sports hall where we invited all prisoners with no mixing issues and even officers who attended on their day off. Again, I understand that not very young person will engage with something like this whilst in custody. This showed me that the officers wanted us to have an opportunity to play on stage, create a sense of community, and hold a room filled with different people. This has stuck with me because of this empowering experience made me pursue my music and now I use it in everyday life and in my current role, teaching music to youth I supervise and work with.

So, after being inside for around 18 months, It was at this point that I was preparing for resettlement and doing a lot more work around release and managing emotions with Danni. We established that due to my conviction, it was proving difficult to get a day release or release on temporary licence (ROTL). However, Danni was so committed to getting me out on some sort of ROTL. After lots of paperwork and pushing on my behalf, she was able to get me on my first ROTL to get some food from the local area, given I was so far away from home. I believe that every child should be granted ROTL before release. I did commit a crime that caused tremendous pain and harm. However, I was not a risk and would not have run, even if I had gone home. This is likely to be the case for many children as they do not have the means to be a flight risk, for example. This is inevitably not the case for other children, and yet I benefitted from prison officers fighting my corner. I witnessed other children struggle with their emotional regulation and intensity or lack of safety that often resides within the carceral space would make prison unbearable for them. It is too easy to see the challenging behaviour and respond with disproportionate power. I could manage my emotions which prevented this for me. I do not however believe this is simply a matter of choice, and these children seem to receive more punishment on top of the loss of liberty. Then, they do not benefit from opportunities and relationships I was afforded. This I believe is what sits behind the reoffending rate of children being consistently and stubbornly high (Hazel & Bateman, 2021). However, Danni's determination and commitment meant she was able to provide what I needed. In turn, she made me realise that this wasn't something she had to do...it was something she chose to do.

Soon after I had a few weeks left and at this point (just like when I had arrived), my emotions, thoughts, and feelings were all over the place. I now realised the quality of some of the relationships I had with Gary and Danni. This is something that I would like every prison officer to understand. We make a connection when you present yourself to us as a human. You can indeed become an authentic connection in that time. When I was due to be released, I honestly found it so hard to say bye to a select few officers. I knew due to restrictions we wouldn't be able to speak again. I wanted to point this out because it is twofold. From my point of view, I found it hard to build those connections. Yet knowing that I wouldn't get to share what I knew were going to be amazing things in my future with them. I found it difficult to understand that from an officer's point of view, they are expected to almost forget about the children they have worked with and developed a relationship with which in my was case 2 years.

Once returning from my ROTL, I blinked, and it was release day. The day I once thought was never going to come, and this was one of my most important days in there. It was on this day that I realised how much progress I had made personally and how prison officers had contributed. I remember waking up with my bags packed and stepping into the unit where I felt a sense of love like I had never felt. There were around ten different education staff that I had great relationships with there. Four officers from the wing I was on, around six officers from different wings, and three officers who weren't even in work that day (including my key worker). They had all come to say bye to me. This is important because even though it doesn't sound much, I come from a place where we struggle to display affection. Therefore, to have a wing full of people say things like 'we are so proud of you' or 'look at the progress you have made' and 'you are going so far.' This showed me that I had people in my life who do believe in me, and I'll always have that even if we never meet again. Things that are often hidden behind prison walls are rarely mentioned when we hear the talk of a broken prison system. The system may well be broken, but the connections and love that develop within the barbed wire are not the issues.

There is one person who I have purposefully waited to mention as I would have mentioned her in practically every sentence as she was a big part of my development. Chanel, my key worker. Now many of you reading this may be assigned to a young person or be a (key worker), and I want you to take a second to appreciate how much impact one key worker can have. Chanel would always take time out of the day to speak to me about my goals, my plans, my family, my friends, my associates, and how I am going to deal with uncomfortable situations, and honestly helped me throughout the entirety of sentence. I can't express how much I appreciated the way she would always make the glass seem half full, rather than half empty. The enthusiasm that she brought onto the wing was infectious. When we're in prison, we need this energy because our lives are challenging. It can be difficult to bond with people that are energy vampires. Again, these skills and qualities are much appreciated inside the prison system as it brings hope and aspiration for young people. Whether you are someone's key worker or not. Whether the young person is presenting 'challenging behaviour' or not. Whether you share the same world views and perspectives or not, be optimistic and try to provide every young person with as many opportunities as possible. Because in the end, you can be the difference!

My Advice from the Inside

Since being released, I have learned many skills and developed many qualities as a practitioner. However, there are some things that I've learnt from my experience of incarceration that have inevitably shaped my practice. When I am working with children and young people now, I take a restorative practice approach of working *with*, not too or for children (Finnis, 2019). I make sure I offer every opportunity to every young person despite their background, offence or presenting behaviours. I take a trauma-informed approach and never underestimate a young person's capabilities. Knowing that I have now obtained employment as an Early Help Practitioner after my predisposition as an incarcerated child creates a belief in me that any child can achieve this if we build hope and believe in them (Inderbitzin, 2012). My personal experience of unexpected interactions, or the being professionally curios and asking questions taught me that this makes a relational difference. Therefore, I apply this approach daily. Reflecting on the effective approaches that professionals took when working with myself and adopting these strategies into my practice. I strive to be present, attuned, relatable, and connected to young people to establish trusting relationships (Brierley, 2021). Very much like Gary, Chanel and Danni did for me. Finally, I have found that no approach is effective if it is not grounded in relationship-based practice (Cherry, 2021).

In terms of giving advice to prison officers, I think it is a lot more than being empathetic, genuine, and approachable. It takes a lot of flexibility, persistence, determination, and drive. From my experience, I believe that most people could be a Good Prison Officer. However, to be a Good Prison Officer, and to not become a stat within the retention rate, this should be considered:

- Some young people have seen things that would make your toes curl. Therefore, never expect to completely understand their world view. That is okay, just be honest!
- Understand that each young person is on their own journey so it's vital to understand their journey before steering them down an unknown path.
- Recognise that young people communicate and navigate situations differently and not let that hinder your judgment of them. To expand, do not let their 'presenting behaviour' determine their opportunities.
- Always ask twice. From my experience, young people will tell you they're fine and things are great even if they're not. Alongside this, remember your asking about their wellbeing that includes relationships inside and outside.
- Remember that some young people come from backgrounds with little love and appreciation; therefore, recognition of their interpretation of relationships is key.
- Finally, remember the glass is always half full!

In my opinion, being a prison officer is such an important role as you are changing lives by connecting with people who may be at their most vulnerable. Therefore, don't just be the person who opens and closes doors. Take time to get to know prisoners and develop relationships with them. Relationships are key to unlocking the potential that sits within every cell on your landing. Thank you for taking this journey with me!

References

Andrews, L. A., Brothers, S. L., Sauvé, J. S., Nangle, D. W., Erdley, C. A., & Hord, M. K. (2019). Fight and flight: Examining putative links between social anxiety and youth aggression. *Aggression and Violent Behavior, 48*, 94–103.

Bateman, T., Hazel, N. (2018). Promoting shifts in personal narratives and providing structures of support: transitions of incarcerated children in England and Wales. In S. O'Neill (Ed.), *Incarcerated youth transitioning back to the community*. Springer. https://doi.org/10.1007/978-981-13-0752-2_11

Brierley, A. (2021). *Connecting with young people in trouble: Risk, relationships and lived experience*. Waterside Press.

Bryan, K., Garvani, G., Gregory, J., & Kilner, K. (2015). Language difficulties and criminal justice: The need for earlier identification. International Journal of Language & Communication Disorders, 50(6), 763–775.

Case, S., & Haines, K. (2021). Abolishing youth justice systems: Children first, offenders nowhere. *Youth Justice, 21*(1), 3–17.

Cherry, L. (2021). *Conversations that make a difference for children and young people: Relationship-focused practice from the frontline*. Routledge.

Creaney, S. (2020). Children's voices—Are we listening? Progressing peer mentoring in the youth justice system. *Child Care in Practice, 26*(1), 22–37.

Duncan, G. J., Magnuson, K., Kalil, A., & Ziol-Guest, K. (2012). The importance of early childhood poverty. *Social Indicators Research, 108*(1), 87–98.

Finnis, M. (2019). *Independent thinking on restorative practice: Building relationships, improving behaviour and creating stronger communities*. Independent Thinking.

Fitzalan Howard, F., & Wakeling, H. (2021). Evaluating the impact of 'rehabilitative adjudications' in four English prisons. *Psychology, Crime & Law, 27*(10), 1010–1031.

Fitzpatrick, C., & Williams, P. (2017). The neglected needs of care leavers in the criminal justice system: Practitioners' perspectives and the persistence of problem (corporate) parenting. Criminology & Criminal Justice, 17(2), 175–191.

Graham, H., & McNeill, F. (2017). Desistance: Envisioning futures. In P. Carlen & L. Ayres França (Eds), *Alternative criminologies* (pp. 433–451). Routledge.

Harriott, P. (2021). No justice without us: Respecting lived experience of the criminal justice system. In G. Smith, T. Hughes, L. Adams, & C. Obijiaku (Eds.), *Democracy in a pandemic* (pp. 75–78). University of Westminster Press.

Hart, R. A. (2008). Stepping back from 'The ladder': Reflections on a model of participatory work with children. In *Participation and learning* (pp. 19–31). Springer.

Hazel, N., & Bateman, T. (2021). Supporting children's resettlement ('reentry') after custody: Beyond the risk paradigm. *Youth Justice, 21*(1), 71–89.

Her Majesties Prison and Probation Service (2021). Prisons Strategy White Paper, Retrieved 17 July 2022, from Prisons Strategy White Paper – GOV.UK (www.gov.uk)

Inderbitzin, M. (2012). Prisons as places of hope and transformative learning. *AI Practitioner, 14*(1). 21–26.

Jaffee, S. R., Bowes, L., Ouellet-Morin, I., Fisher, H. L., Moffitt, T. E., Merrick, M. T., & Arseneault, L. (2013). Safe, stable, nurturing relationships break the intergenerational cycle of abuse: A prospective nationally representative cohort of children in the United Kingdom. *Journal of Adolescent Health, 53*(4), S4–S10.

Kenny, T., & Webster, S. (2015). Experiences of prison officers delivering five minute interventions at HMP/YOI Portland. *NOMS Analytical Summary.*

Lenkens, M. (2022). More than a Mirror: Mechanisms of experiential peer support for young people engaging in criminal behaviour. Public Health, 2022-04-26, SDG 16 – Peace, Justice and Strong Institutions, Erasmus University Rotterdam.

Lenkens, M., Nagelhout, G. E., Schenk, L., Sentse, M., Severiens, S., Engbersen, G., & van Lenthe, F. J. (2021). 'I (really) know what you mean'. Mechanisms of experiential peer support for young people with criminal behavior: A qualitative study. *Journal of Crime and Justice, 44*(5), 535–552.

Lyons-Ruth, K. (1996). Attachment relationships among children with aggressive behavior problems: The role of disorganized early attachment patterns. *Journal of Consulting and Clinical Psychology, 64*(1), 64.

Maruna, S. (2001). Making good (p. 86). American Psychological Association.

Maruna, S., & Ramsden, D. (2004). Living to tell the tale: redemption narratives, shame management, and offender rehabilitation. In A. Lieblich, D. P. McAdams, & R. Josselson (Eds.), Healing plots: The narrative basis of psychotherapy (pp. 129–149). American Psychological Association. https://doi.org/10.1037/10682-007

McMurran, M. (2009). Motivational interviewing with offenders: A systematic review. *Legal and Criminological Psychology, 14*(1), 83–100.

McNeill, F., & Maruna, S. (2007). Giving up and giving back: Desistance, generativity, and social work with offenders. *Developments in Social Work With Offenders, 48,* 224–339.

McNeill, F., Farrall, S., Lightowler, C., & Maruna, S. (2012). 'How and why people stop offending: Discovering desistance.' *Insights Evidence Summary to Support Social Services in Scotland.* Institute for Research and Innovation in Social Services.

Peer Power/Youth Justice Board (2021). *Co-creation and participation in practice project.* Peer Power/YJB.

Presser, L., & Sandberg, S. (2019). Narrative criminology as critical criminology. *Critical Criminology, 27,* 131–143. https://doi.org/10.1007/s10612-019-09437-9

Rotherham Youth Justice Service Peer Review – Final Report (March 2022), Youth Justice Sector Improvement Partnership, Retrieved 23 August 2022, from [Agenda item – Rotherham Youth Offending Team. HMIP Inspection Action Plan Progress Report – Rotherham Council].

Rowe, M., & Soppitt, S. (2014). 'Who you gonna call?' The role of trust and relationships in desistance from crime. *Probation Journal, 61*(4), 397–412.

Spencer, N. (2003). Social, economic, and political determinants of child health. *Pediatrics, 112*(Supplement_3), 704–706.

Steiner, B., & Wooldredge, J. (2018). Prison officer legitimacy, their exercise of power, and inmate rule breaking. *Criminology, 56*(4), 750–779.

Szifris, K., Fox, C., & Bradbury, A. (2018). A realist model of prison education, growth, and desistance: A new theory. *Journal of Prison Education and Reentry, 5*(1), 41–62.

Tampubolon, G. (2015). Growing up in poverty, growing old in infirmity: The long arm of childhood conditions in Great Britain. *PLoS One, 10*(12), e0144722.

Wickham, S., Anwar, E., Barr, B., Law, C., & Taylor-Robinson, D. (2016). Poverty and child health in the UK: Using evidence for action. *Archives of Disease in Childhood, 101*(8), 759–766.

Wright, S., Liddle, M., & Goodfellow, P. (2016). Young offenders and trauma: Experience and impact: A practitioner's guide.

8 Relationships Are the Agents of Change

James Docherty, Prison Number - 24722

Who Am I?

I am a father, a son, a brother, a mentor, a closed-mouth friend. I am a person who has both professional and personal experience in navigating the care and criminal justice system. I made it out because the by-product of understanding human suffering is compassion – and compassion is a verb. People took action to help.

I work for the Scottish Violence Reduction Unit (VRU). I have worked on various innovative VRU projects mentoring people with convictions seeking to re-create their lives. I helped co-create the award-winning Street and Arrow project modelled on the largest gang rehabilitation project in the world 'Homeboy Industries' based in Los Angeles. I am a trauma-responsive practitioner who advocates strongly for change and awareness in how we address the hidden cost of untreated trauma and Adverse Childhood Experiences (ACE's) in our society (Felitti et al., 1998).

I am a public speaker and workshop facilitator who has travelled to Scotland teaching and campaigning publicly on how to enable the change we all seek in navigating people away from the justice system, preventing trauma, and facilitating healing and rehabilitation – with the sole aim of preventing more victims. A large part of my work has been on primary prevention, which led me to bring an internationally renowned speaker, trauma, attachment, and addiction expert Dr Gabor Mate to Scotland in 2019 for a national conference in partnership with ACE-Aware Nation (see Walsh, 2020). Primary prevention is often the forgotten piece in navigating people away from the justice system. I am a person who believes that the solution to how we immunise people from most social dysfunction lies in how we raise our babies. In the early rearing environment. Our social responsibility means we need to get it right for families to get it right for

DOI: 10.4324/9781003349747-8

the children. Childhood trauma is an intergeneration public health and social problem (Lambert et al., 2017). No longer can we blame, shame, or disgrace parents.

Sometimes the disease metaphor is apt to explain the public health strategy in primary prevention. We know that Polio was not eradicated by treatment, it was ended by primary prevention. A vaccine! Like polio, the prison pipeline will not be ended or even reduced much by punishing people or fear tactics. You simply cannot punish trauma with a better way of being in the world. It's already a punishing enough experience. It will be in the form of ending poverty, creating relational wealth as outlined by Andi in his chapter, a new kind of public health approach on educating parents, creating optimal child-rearing conditions and dosing down the stress across the whole culture. I fundamentally believe it is a fireside-out solution! Mother Teresa is quoted as saying; 'What can you do to promote world peace? Go home and love your family' (Bojaxhiu, 2003). Even this wee woman knew all those years ago, that the solution to this was from the fireside out. So, it's everyone's business. Secondary prevention and tertiary must always be a working part of what we do. As it all points to the primary solution of how we raise our children. Whether we like it or not, prisoners have children, so we need to get it right for them, to get it right for the children. They are innocent.

I work in an Advisory capacity at Community Justice Scotland. My role is a cross team functional post that aims to ensure all work is fully aligned to Community Justice Scotland values and is community focused. I am responsible for increasing knowledge across the teams and advising on approaches to strategies, projects, and priorities. I also lead on community-based lived experience events, along with a wide range of public speaking and engagement activity. In all my time in prevention work, I have never come across an individual in the justice system that wasn't reporting a history of adverse childhood experiences. So, who I am in this context is about preventing that and enabling the process of recovery and healing from its effects? It only ever happens in the context of healthy relationships! In May 2022 in support of our vision for a fair and compassionate justice system in Scotland, and in partnership with the Scottish Prison Service, Sustainable Interventions Supporting Change Outside (SISCO), Trauma Informed Lawyers, Community Justice Scotland, Violence Reduction Unit, and ACE Aware Nation, we welcomed Fritzi Hortsman, founder of The Compassion Prison Project (CPP) in America, to Scotland to facilitate CPD workshops in several Scottish Prisons. With the sole aim of raising awareness in how we create trauma-informed prisons and communities. The focus was on the lives of the men and women living and working in these prisons and how trauma can gravely affect their lives. We continue to widen the circle of compassion.

My Prison Experience

I could give you the story of chaos, violence, drugs, and organised crime, the who's who at the zoo narrative we are often fed in crime novels, biographies, and TV. It is a familiar story often told and yet betrays the emotional and psychological underpinnings of what sucks people into the justice system. So, more importantly, I want to focus on the causes and conditions, what prevents it, what enables us to stop seeing the same faces cycling in our justice systems – and to recognise we can all contribute to reducing recidivism in our own unique way. It has been a truism of my life to discover that relationships and not individualism are the prerequisite to all change. People used to say to me when I walked away from a life of crime and chaos that you must have had a massive inner drive and determination to renounce it all and walk out into the unknown for the life you have now? But I always tell people, that it's a question that doesn't interest me. The question they should be really asking is, 'who was there for you, and who is there for you now?' Because nothing happens out-with the mirror of relationship. If it was not for the relationships afforded to me on my journey I would have turned back to the familiar road of chaos, because I had people on it. My willingness would have run out on the road to redemption if it was only ever walked alone. Because we humans are social animals, we are not built to be alone. We do not fare well in isolation.

The great spiritual teacher Jiddu Krishnamurti said, 'Action has meaning only in relationship, and without an understanding relationship, action on any level will only breed conflict. The understanding of relationship is infinitely more important than the search for any plan of action' (Krishnamurti, 2013). This is a quote that deeply resonates with me because this understanding is a 'must' regarding managing the complexities of looking after people in our care, in any setting. To recognise the power differential in relationships as people navigate the justice system is both critical to safety and mutuality. I entered the adult prison system as a 15-year-old child. I was already well known to the children's panel and social work system. A bed couldn't be found in secure care for me, so I was taken to Scotland's notorious Barlinnie prison, Scotland's busiest establishment.

One night there, and then onwards to Longriggend high-security young offenders' prison (now closed). I spent a few days here in the schoolboy's unit until a bed was found in Kerelaw secure unit (now closed). At no point in the journey did it occur to me, I was a child being propelled around a system devoid of an understanding of relationship. I was strip searched and then 'I was left in the dug box' in Barlinnie reception for six hours. That small I could lie long way on the floor and sleep! Maybe they kept me there until the system worked out what to do with a child in an adult establishment. In any stressful event, or under duress human beings find marvellous ways of coping – one of mine was the use of humour. If I could keep the focus off me 'on the Bar bus' as it was known, the adult prisoners would be distracted from my vulnerability. I spent the journey in the 'beast box' just because I was a child. My fear was the prisoners would think I was a sex offender 'whit ye dain in the beasts box wee man?' everyone laughed. I was terrified I'd be attacked; I knew what happened to people who were sex offenders in these places. My uncle had been active in both Barlinnie and the Glenochil prison riots and he took great delight in telling me what they did to these people when they could.

Who came up with that name I don't know, but it was common knowledge who was kept in these boxes with a small 5 by 8-inch window away from the other prisoners on transport from Glasgow Sheriff court to Barlinnie. The Police ran the whole operation. I did not like the Police; with good reason. A belief reinforced further when I was assaulted by the officer on exiting the bus for using humour to slaughter everything, I could find wrong with his appearance. The whole bus was in hysterics, for a moment in time it was a welcome distraction, yet it left me black and blue. I reckon I weighed around seven stone at the time. The power differential was enormous. I had chosen what the holocaust survivor Victor Frankl called: 'The last of the human freedoms, to choose one's own attitude under any given set of circumstances' (Frankl, 1990). Maybe if the officer had understood my plight, he would have understood, 'my attitude was a coping mechanism, just a frightened wee boy' and not taken it so personally. His assault on me was by no means the worst experience at the hands of authorities, but it has left the largest emotional and psychological imprint. I can still remember his face to the day. I was utterly at the mercy of these adults with no sense of escape. The only reason I share the experience is because, if we really understand that relationships are the agents of change, then we must understand and accept that recidivism cannot take place under these conditions.

Prison is about loss of liberty; it should never be about loss of humanity. I believe if the truth is to be well served, it cannot push people into polarised positions. Everyone should feel secure, respected, and connected no matter where they are in life. Even prison. The moral high ground is not a place to stand on, it's lonely away up there being so righteously perfect and plus not many hold the position in my experience! There lies a problem of thinking prison holds bad people, and good people keep them there as this overthinking towards security can distract us from understanding that safe relationships are fundamentally what creates a safer society. There's a Solzhenitsyn quote which I love, and quote frequently in trying to get us humans to see our own hypocrisy. I think it enables us to recognise our own liabilities, our own shortcomings, prejudices, or whatever you want to call it and know that there is not a paragon of virtue among us human beings. The quote goes like this:

> If only there were evil people somewhere insidiously committing evil deeds, and it were necessary only to separate them from the rest of us and destroy them. But the line dividing good and evil cuts through the heart of every human being. And who is willing to destroy a piece of his own heart?
>
> (Hogan & Lies, 2011 p.234).

The trouble with making the distinction of 'good people' and the 'bad people' as Solzhenistsyn says, is the focus is external – it stops us looking inwards at our own character flaws. For me this is one of the great enemies in understanding relationships. It is easy to alienate, exclude, other or treat a human being differently when we see them as evil or in some way different from our friends or family.

On entering Lonriggend YOI, I was again processed. A prison officer looked up at me while taking my details and said, 'what are you doing in here wee man, your too good looking to be in here?' I smiled and said, 'let me oot then?' He laughed! What a decent big guy I thought. Just a small statement, but big to me. Someone was seeing a positive in me. Because the truth is I hated myself. I was to encounter him many times as I navigated Lonriggend as a youth and he was always respectful. It was always reciprocated. Funny that, us humans are always apt to give what we receive!

Lonriggend reception also had 'dug boxes' although a little bigger, not much. I was strip searched again and then onwards to the Schoolboys Hall. I spent three days here and was shipped to secure care. I spent the next year in Kerelaw. I arrived in prison handcuffs; my wrists that small they had to put a metal filler in them to stop them falling off my wrists. Standing in the staff office the other children looked on with curiosity. Little did I know I had just entered an establishment that was to become subject of an independent abuse enquiry (see Frizzell, 2009).

Although restraint was a feature of my time there, I never questioned it as it was normal to me. You fight or kick off, you get carted. My belief was, 'your basically in a children's prison James and this is how it goes, trust no one.' My experience was that anytime staff laid hands on me it was for fighting with another resident. The extent of the force used and time in restraint and subsequent isolation from my peers was a symptom of a system devoid of understanding relationships. These experiences represented a type of relational rupture which when understood in its entirety must always move to relational repair. But it was never explored, and never repaired. The staff don't know why I was fighting, or what was the trigger into conflict. I navigated the whole system with Complex Post Traumatic Stress Disorder (CPTSD), and no one noticed (see Redican et al., 2021).

It never occurred to me that on entering the system young, it was against my will, that I was already full of internal distress. A dynamic also compounded by the fact I was already a deeply traumatised young man who's mirror of relationship was warped by my early caregiving experiences. This left me with a deep fear of authority, some of which was valid and compounded by how I was treated. A fear that manifested itself in distrust of adults, and contempt for anyone in a uniform. Even the lollipop man was a threat to my self-efficacy and autonomy as a child. 'I'll decide when I cross the road, not you,' was my thinking after leaving a traumatised family system that morning. My attitude was, I am running my life, not you, a self-reliance being built before it's time. I call it Frank Sinatra syndrome 'I'll do it my way.' People in the prison system are often misdiagnosed and misunderstood. One of my irks is that people perceive prisoners as resilient, when the truth is its mostly survival. Resilient people bounce back to health very quickly, not in and out of prison.

Judith Lewis Herman in her book, Trauma and Recovery: The Aftermath of Violence – From Domestic Abuse and Political Terror explains this dynamic perfectly when stating that

> many abused children cling to the hope that growing up will bring escape and freedom. But the personality formed in the environment of coercive control is not well adapted to adult life. The survivor is left with fundamental problems in basic trust, autonomy, and initiative. She approaches the task of early adulthood, establishing independence and intimacy, burdened by major impairments in self-care, in cognition and in memory, in identity, and

> in the capacity to form stable relationships. She is still a prisoner
> of her childhood; attempting to create a new life, she reencounters
> the trauma.
>
> (Herman, 2015, p. 231).

It's like, I could not wait to get older to run my life, and then when I got there, I didn't know what to do. I was too scared to ask. No wonder authority figures scratched their head in bewilderment and frustration on what to do with me. It is very difficult to help a person who has built a wall around them. Sometimes we fail to recognise that our best efforts in a punitive system add bricks to that wall and not foundations to the bridge that enables them to access a pathway into healing and recovery.

Is it any wonder why we medicate and manage these symptoms rather than address the causes and conditions? Hardened criminals and hardened prison staff are not that much different. They are often both mirrors of each other. A hardness created in response to a harsh environment. It is a bit like the callous on your hands when you go to the gym. It's developed not chosen to protect your hands. So, it's always worth exploring what creates the conditions that harden people and recognise that beneath the harsh exterior is a softness, always available, yet often undiscovered. I left care at 16 years old, with no aftercare. Straight back to the community and chaos ensued. I was to spend the next nine years cycling in and out the justice system, until I met a person with lived experience of recovery who changed the course of my life. He had deviated from his treatment plan on weekend leave from rehab to come and tell me why I needed to go to rehab. I listened intently as he told me about his recovery. It was self-evident, I knew him, and he was not the same person. That is why he had my attention. He was an agent of change. I took his advice; I took a course of action. I found myself in the same rehab, healing was messy business, but I was surrounded by people who had solved the drink and drug problem.

I felt safe in there, they got me, they also challenged my old ideas, my faulty belief systems, and my unhealthy coping mechanisms. They nurtured my childhood wounds and showed me a level of compassion and acceptance I rarely see anywhere else. See that's the thing, we heal in relationships. I was free… at last. I came home determined to let the world know about childhood trauma. Little did I know where that determination to help others would take me. It's always bothered me that I spent all that time in the justice system and that it took lived experienced therapists and doctors in recovery to give me a full knowledge of the addictive illness and the trauma that underpinned it. What a waste of money and resource. I was on the inside looking out, and now I am on the outside looking in. Two internal frames of reference that are unique to my role in this system.

My Advice from the inside

The science of toxic stress in childhood and the understanding of trauma has swept Scotland in recent years and this has radically changed the lens on how we view people navigating the justice system (Ford et al., 2019; Shonkoff et al., 2012). It is now astoundingly obvious that the adaptations to a childhood marred by neglect, and abuse derails healthy development and can alter an individual's perception of the world. These adaptations although normal in response to these abnormal circumstances do not often meet social expectations of behaviour, and when that happens, they often find themselves in contact with the justice system. The search for awareness and best practice in working with others from traumatic backgrounds has been the greatest challenge in my working life. The discovery of my own trauma was the sudden realisation that traditional service delivery approaches had added to my troubles, never instilling hope, or demonstrating the compassion needed to connect to an individual looking for a way out of a bad situation.

I have always valued the practice and effectiveness of 'Lived Experience' as part of the multi-faceted solution to the issues and barriers people face in often overcoming life-long adversities. The therapeutic value of people sharing how they have found a solution to any life problem is without parallel in my experience. That innate human ability to cultivate hope and meaning in the lives of people who are still trying to solve life problems, is one of the most effective tools I know for supporting change. What I feel is misunderstood about lived experience is – everyone has it, but we don't all use it, and it's not just attributed to mental health, addictions, or offending as its often perceived in many mainstream professional roles. It's just about taking your 'whole self' to work. Not just similar experiences.

It's fundamentally about empathy, compassion, and humility. If that means only shared experience, that's okay. If it helps another human being out of a bad situation, or betters their life circumstances or cultivates hope, then let's celebrate it. I was told about the officer who used to run the recovery café with SISCO in Barlinnie. I met him, an amazing man. The prisoners totally loved him. He had shared with them his pain at losing a family member to addiction and that was why he took up the post. That's bringing your whole self to work. Making trauma informed practice a working part of your mind is fundamentally about self-care. It allows you to think differently about how you serve the people who access you for support in your personal as well as your work life. It is very easy to forget that in five minutes you may be about to work with an individual who may feel unwanted, unlovable, angry, broken, and full of shame. Even a simple, how are you mate, when you open the door is social connection, being consistently decent with human beings will always be reciprocated. Us and them cannot survive in an atmosphere of mutuality. So, for me trauma awareness is critical to the helping role. A good reason being – if we are not trauma aware, we can run the risk of re-traumatisation.

If our approach to individuals is not based on the understanding of trauma, vulnerabilities, or the triggers of trauma survivors we can and will unwittingly exacerbate the wounds that people carry. Wounds that even they are not aware of yet. It could be the difference between engaging in a service or not. Life and death. Yes, that's how serious I believe this issue is. I heard a story recently of a Police Officer who attended a suicide. He found a note in the persons house, and it said, 'I am walking to the bridge, if someone smiles at me on the way or stops to say hello, I will not jump!' Prison staff are faced with suicide regularly. A smile or a hello that morning might be the difference in a person feeling his worth in this world and staying around to know it for sure.

In my work I don't need to know a person's history to be able to cultivate compassion. I just assume everyone is wounded and walking an untold pain. My experience of prison is that it's a highly stressful environment. Most prisoners are overcompensating to cover up their fear. Fear does not make you a hard man, but it can make you dangerous. People who have a wounded stress response system are the classic Meerkat scanning the environment for threat, exaggerated swagger, and loud booming bravado as Max outlined in his chapter. It's all fear based. An overcompensation to cover up low self-esteem and low self-worth. You know what I am talking about, you see it every day when the doors open, and prisoners mix. There is an energy in a prison you do not find in any other setting. It's the collective overactive stress response you're feeling when all those doors open.

After a while you become conditioned to it, the abnormal becomes normal. Therefore, I believe prisons should offer psycho-educational programmes on toxic stress and teach tools on how to regulate the nervous system. As part of the problem with many people in prison is, they never had full access to the cortex at the time of the crime. It was only partially accessible. It is why when you sit down and talk with them, they say of course I know it was wrong, of course I know it was unhealthy. yes, I know it has caused harm, yes. I have remorse. Of course, I know the consequences of it all. But why did you do it? I wasn't really thinking at the time! And he or she is often right. The cognitive functioning due to childhood trauma is often offline at the time of the crime due to stress activation.

It's why we call it the autonomic nervous system – it is automatic! It's why in a debrief after a prison incident that activated the stress response its often reported to staff that they have done something they have no memory of doing. Because they are in fight or flight. The cortex goes offline. Therefore, I believe we need to teach prisoners everything we know about trauma and adverse childhood experiences – so that the individual feels empowered to become a collaborator in their own healing rather than the recipient of the traditional offending behaviour programmes that enable progression through a system. Every relapse into old behaviour I have seen that halts a person's progress through the system can be attributed to one thing – stress! And please don't worry about opening the can of worms' myth, it's already open.

Giving people information that helps them make sense of their internal world and the tools to dose down the stress response creates more choice as people have larger access to the cortex. The part of our brain we all take for granted. The part of our brain where true choice is accessed. Please make self-care a central feature in your own life, your family deserve the best of you, not the stressed you. Take the time to assess your own and everyone's potential for trauma in their past. The good news is that it can heal, it's never a lost cause. That's where the hope is. The pace and pressures of modern services can make it difficult to implement a trauma responsive approach. You'll make mistakes, we all do. I have made many, but there is always opportunity for repair, it's necessary work. The more trauma-responsive we are, the more effective our services and relationships will be. It all begins with awareness. If I can leave this one thing in your awareness, let it be this quote from Dr Paul Tournier, 'No one can develop freely in this world and find a full life without feeling understood by at least one person' (Tournier, 1967). You can be that person as The Good Prison Officer.

References

Bojaxhiu, A. G. (2003). Mother Teresa, Wikipedia, available online [Mother Teresa - Wikipedia, the free encyclopedia. Retrieved 12 September 2022, from zubiaga.org)

Felitti, V. J., Anda, R. F., Nordenberg, D., Williamson, D. F., Spitz, A. M., Edwards, V., & Marks, J. S. (1998). Relationship of childhood abuse and house-hold dysfunction to many of the leading causes of death in adults: The adverse childhood experiences (ACE) study. *American Journal of Preventive Medicine, 14*(4), 245–258.

Ford, K., Barton, E., Newbury, A., Hughes, K., Bezeczky, Z., Roderick, J., & Bellis, M. (2019). Understanding the prevalence of adverse childhood experi-ences (ACEs) in a male offender population in Wales: The prisoner ACE survey. Public Health Wales, Bangor University.

Frankl, V. (1990). *Human in search of meaning.* Progress.

Frizzell, E. (2009). Independent Inquiry into Abuse at Kerelaw Residential School and Secure Unit. Jointly commissioned by the Scottish Government and Glasgow City Council. Available at Independent Inquiry into Abuse at Kerelaw Residential School and Secure Unit (iriss.org.uk) Accessed 12/08/22.

Herman, J. L. (2015). *Trauma and recovery: The aftermath of violence–from domestic abuse to political terror.* Hachette.

Hogan, M. M., & Lies, J. (2011). HISTORY (1933–1948), University of Portland

Krishnamurti, J. (2013). *The first and last freedom.* Random House.

Lambert, H. K., Meza, R., Martin, P., Fearey, E., & McLaughlin, K. A. (2017). Childhood trauma as a public health issue. In *Evidence-based treatments for trauma related disorders in children and adolescents* (pp. 49–66). Springer.

Redican, E., Nolan, E., Hyland, P., Cloitre, M., McBride, O., Karatzias, T., & Shevlin, M. (2021). A systematic literature review of factor analytic and mixture models of ICD-11 PTSD and CPTSD using the international trauma question-naire. *Journal of Anxiety Disorders, 79*, 102381.

Shonkoff, J. P., Garner, A. S., Siegel, B. S., Dobbins, M. I., Earls, M. F., & McGuinn, L. (2012). The lifelong effects of early childhood adversity and toxic stress. *Pediatrics, 129*(1), e232–e246.

Tournier, P. (1967). *To understand each other.* Westminster John Knox Press.

Walsh, G. M. (2020). The arrival of the ACEs movement in Scotland: Policy entrepreneurship and critical activist responses. *Scottish Affairs, 29*(4), 456–474.

9 Time for Change

Andi Brierley

Time for Change

Throughout the chapters of this book, you have heard the voices of ex-prisoners in various professional roles articulate what they believe is required for the prison services in England, Wales, Scotland, and Jersey to make a positive impact on the 'stubbornly high reoffending rates' (HMPPS, 2021, p. 7). Providing examples of good practice, as well as areas for development. There doesn't seem to be one approach, style, or practice model of effectively caring for prisoners which have been established in previous research demonstrating prison officer typologies of care (see Tait, 2011). However, as these chapters have demonstrated, the inclusion of the voice and perspectives of prisoners and ex-prisoners can make a positive contribution to the way care in prison is both delivered and received. To ensure there is a collaborative approach, our recommendations will align with or enhance the Prison Strategy White Paper (HMPPS, 2021).

This final chapter is our collective effort to take an innovative approach to reduce crime and developing rehabilitative prisons. To provide more evidence to illustrate the value of implementing these recommendations, we have taken a step back from the local picture to observe other countries with proven track records of reducing recidivism. Places like Norway and other Scandinavian countries have had a positive impact on recidivism resulting from a focus on job training programmes, encouraging employment, and discouraging crime (Bhuller et al., 2020; Ugelvik, 2016). A clear focus on desistance and a humane prison system that treats prisoners as human beings is evidence of shaking off any residue of the 'Nothing Works' doctrine (Martinson, 1974). A doctrine that developed after a review of over 200 US prison rehabilitative programmes undertaken in the 1970s concluding that 'with few and isolated exceptions, the rehabilitative efforts that have

DOI: 10.4324/9781003349747-9

been reported so far have had no appreciable effect on recidivism' (Martinson, 1974, p. 25). Developing an alteration in criminal justice policy meant 'criminology experienced a paradigm shift in its underlying set of operating assumptions' (Cullen & Gendreau, 2019, p. 33). The Nordic countries are seemingly leading the way in presenting a new 'what works' approach to crime. Reducing crime through focusing on treating prisoners as people that will reintegrate as community members, as opposed to social stigma, retribution, and further punishment upon release through exclusion from the labour market (Henley, 2014).

The Nordic countries' approach to responding to crime in this way has been described as 'Nordic Exceptionalism' by researchers from Anglophone countries (Bruhn et al., 2017). Norway has seen a reduction in reoffending rates from 80% in the 1980s to 20–25% today (Høidal, 2018). The focus of their 'exceptionalism' derives from their leading efforts to have low incarceration rates and humane prison conditions which do not eradicate the pains of prison. However, they must surely ease them (Johnsen et al., 2011). Research exploring the prisoner, officer relationships in Norway's prisons found that these relationships were better in smaller Norwegian prisons (Johnsen et al., 2011). Less people in prison making for a more relational prison experience, even within an exceptional country. Although on closer analysis, the argument that Nordic prisons are indeed exceptional is not straight forward. Thomas Ugelvik (2016) explored whether the Nordic Exceptionalism argument holds up through contemporary Norwegian research. Arguing in his conclusion that 'whether it is correct to say that Norwegian prisons themselves are welfare institutions or that they should be described as penal institutions with close ties to the welfare state agencies may depend on your perspective' (p.17). However, accepting that if recidivism rates is a trusted measure (which many would argue is not), the Norwegian prison system still produces a relatively low-rate post custody.

These international examples of exceptionalism alongside the evidence in this book would suggest that smaller prisons, more officers, less workloads, more interactions, and a focus on staff – prisoner relationships would create a community like feel to prison which can be achieved. It would take allowing prison officers the time to become those *good prison officers* described by Liebling et al. (1999, p. 83) as officers that don't 'use force, but get things done.' With all this in mind, within the Prison Strategy White Paper for Prison's in England and Wales, there is a commitment to deliver '18,000 additional modern places by the mid 2020's' (HMPPS, 2021, p. 12). In England and Wales therefore, we have a contrasting ideology of the use of prisons to our exceptional neighbours. The prison numbers in England and Wales have indeed doubled over the past three decades (Turner & Peacock, 2017). Demonstrating that instead of reducing prison numbers which evidence suggests reduces crime, our governments seem to be responding to a predicted trajectory that even more people will be sent to prison. As a result, HMPPS are making a commitment to recruit '5,000 additional prison officers' (HMPPS, 2021, p. 59). Five thousand more officers for 18,000 more prisoners indicates that the ratio per prisoner remains the same, even though the institutions become larger. We argue that this is a very worrying game of trying to have rehabilitation on the cheap within an overly punitive system which will not likely create safer communities, nor reduce victims in the long run.

Our collective concern as a team of professionals with prisoner experience is that these numbers will not create safer prisons, but less safer prisons because the government fail to recourse prisons to respond to this increase in prison numbers. We would like to see higher ratios of prison officers and these numbers above seem to maintain status quo of around one operational professional to every four prisoners according to the HMPPS (2021) data. The chapters in this book highlight that prison officers can indeed develop relational spaces with prisoners when they are provided the relational context to spend time with prisoners, get to know prisoners and understand prisoners needs. In my role as a University Teacher teaching on the Unlocked Masters programme, I have had many conversations with officers that acknowledge the lack of time and resource to achieve the outcomes they set themselves when joining the Unlocked mission of rehabilitation.

Charlie Taylor, the Chief Inspector of prisons discussed prison officer retention recently. He stated: 'As much as of an issue as recruitment is retention. People just aren't staying around. Perhaps that's because they come into prisons without a full understanding of what the job entails' (Inside Time, 2022 para.1). This issue of retention cannot be seen as mutually exclusive to reoffending rates as evidenced in the chapters of this book. Prison officers are indeed the agents of safety and desistance within the prison context. Therefore, this retention matter is a major issue for public safety as outlined by Max Dennehy. It has been suggested in literature that increasing staffing levels in prison can be a way of manipulating the working context to reduce stress levels of prison officers (Marzano & Adler, 2007). As the authors of each chapter have highlighted, the more present, attuned, and connected the officers are to us as prisoners, the more likely they are to obtain trust, or consent to improve the behaviour of us as prisoners (Crewe, 2011). Inadvertently, over stressed prison officers are going to be less relational and unable to meet the needs of prisoners, which is unlikely to positively impact on reoffending rates. We do not see this as being complicated. However, this increase in prison staff is likely to have financial implications (Marzano & Adler, 2007) so it may be important for more involvement of people with prison experience in public discourse and literature.

In a study exploring prison officer burnout in the UK, researchers found that 'prison officers face a number of environmental (e.g., overcrowding) and occupational (e.g., understaffing) stressors' (Lovell & Brown, 2017, p. 721). We are creating a prison context that burns prison officers out, then wonder why officers are unable to meet the needs of and support prisoners. It is not a case of making prison life easier for prisoners, but an issue of not creating very unsafe environments which is very unlikely to destress prisoners so that desistance can take place. The serious risks of understaffing have also been identified in a study of prison officers as a reason for them not being off sick (Kinman et al., 2019). This pressure on officers needs more discussion at a political level as the health of prison officers is central to reducing reoffending post prison. Peter Dawson, the head of Prison Reform Trust recently stated that 'we know what happens when there are too many prisoners and too few prison staff—more violence, self-harm and suicide, and less rehabilitation. That is where the government's love affair with imprisonment is leading. It's time to think again' (Prison Reform Trust, 2022, para.4). Maybe we need to rethink the way prison looks if we are to continue with current levels of staffing and ourselves embed a principle of *normality* (Labutta, 2016). More open prisons for lower-level offending and revolving door, persistent people that offend could alleviate the pressure on prison officers to staff secure prisons because less secure prisons need less resource.

In Norway for example, they have a *normality* principle as they see 'the punishment as the restriction of liberty; no other rights have been removed by the sentencing court. Therefore, the sentenced individual has all the same rights as all others who live in Norway' (Høidal, 2018, p.61; see also Mjåland et al., 2022). It is difficult to expect British politicians to align themselves with such a principle within British culture when populist views and media depictions of a lenient justice system sway public opinion (Mason, 2006). However, the lead needs to be taken by politicians if we are to expect a change in culture and an improvement of this very expensive and inadequate punishment apparatus (Johns, 2017). We as authors may have varying views on whether prison is an effective response to crime overall. This is not dissimilar to academics in the field of criminology. One consistent theme that comes through loud and clear from each chapter is that developing a relational community feel to prison officer practice is likely to impact positively on recidivism rates. There is clear learning from the Nordic model of having a key principle such as normality to ensure that restriction of liberty is the sole punishment and prison replicates as much of a normal community as possible. This would be a step in the right direction. This doesn't come at a cost of security, but a change in how we see many that enter our prison system. However, in the long run this would likely mean officers would be less likely to burn out because they would get far more job satisfaction when making a difference to the lives of those they care for.

Another key theme was the youth estate having extensive training around Child First Principles of treating children as children, developing a pro-social identity, participation, co-production, and to a less extent diversion (Case & Haines, 2021). Children are not small adults. There is a capacity and culpability difference between children and adults which should impact on how they are responded to and held accountable by the justice system. Research is currently highlighting that we are seemingly criminalising many children with neurodiverse needs that are not understood by education and youth justice (Day, 2022). All prison officers working with children must have child first principles at the forefront of practice for these reasons. It is not child friendly to hold children in prisons that replicate adults, just because they are granted more resources which create a higher officer to prisoner ratio. This book highlights pockets of good practice. However, more needs to be done to ensure children in custody do not experience officers that fail to understand the diverse needs of justice involved *children*. Moreover, the impact of adverse childhood experience, toxic stress, and childhood trauma on behaviour which has been stressed as imperative by me, Kierra, Devon, Dan, and James.

Both Kierra and Devon explained how those officers that understood them, their abilities and worldviews made a difference to their road through custody to desistance. The child first principles adopted by the YJB give the Youth Custody Service (YCS) and HMPPS an opportunity to embed this knowledge into the heart of their training for Youth Justice Workers (YJW) (Case & Haines, 2021). The current training package delivered to YJWs is a level four qualification. According to the Youth Custody Service (YCS) website, this covers 'speech, language and communication needs, and the essential skills for child protection and safeguarding' (YCS, 2020). We believe that the evidence base behind the child first principles should be a central tenet of training for any professional working with justice involved children in a custodial setting. That it requires a particular focus to drive 'improved moral quality' with current knowledge of the impact of trauma on people in prisons (Auty et al., 2022, p. 19).

A combination of introducing such specific principles into training for officers working with children, women, *and* men, developing humane policies and investment in building relationships between prisoners and officers which have been implemented in Scandinavia; alongside incorporating the perspectives in these chapters and more books of this kind would improve the lives of prisoners by creating safe spaces in prisons. It is not a case of 'punishing less, but punishing better' (Shammas, 2014, p. 120). The authors of each chapter were selected as they had experienced youth custody, multiple sentences, school exclusion, or addiction as these social determinants represent a large proportion of prisoners that have scarcely experienced safe lives prior to entering custody. They do not represent the voice of all prisoners. However, the experiences of these social factors render them close to what are the most vulnerable groups of prisoners. They represent the lives of many that maintain the stubbornly high reoffending rates because of their exposure to adverse social conditions way before they entered the prison estate, which is not the case for all prisoners. A group that has a good understanding of how prison impacts on the future behaviour of those with such experiences.

As a group, we believe that increasing prison officer numbers alone is unlikely to develop a rehabilitative culture. The cultural change needs to have focussed training for officers and embed the lived experience realities into the heart of officer training. I have witnessed lots of discussions over a lengthy career in various aspects of the justice system when I have thought 'this discussion would be different if more people with lived experience were involved.' It is more than inclusion and diversity; it is developing a full picture from multiple perspectives to enhance the justice system. This book demonstrates that we as ex-prisoners have the commitment and dedication, not excluding the knowledge and expertise to contribute to developing a more humane prison system. If this book and recommendations are not explored and considered by government, policy makers and ministers, we can only wonder whether the prison system is indeed focussed on shifting prison culture for the better. The prison system that the authors of this book experienced over decades has often become a pawn within a political game of punishment and rehabilitation. Often punished by the system but supported by relationships.

The prisons in England, Wales, Scotland, and Jersey have enlightened all the authors of this book with varying insights of care which we have offered as narratives to help instigate change. Each author experienced prison in a different way. All would agree that although it was not all bad, with some level of reform, our health and wellbeing would have improved. In exploring the structural determinants of prison health, De Viggiani (2007) found that 'the notion of a 'healthy prison' remains something of an oxymoron without significant reform of the way prisons are managed and offenders are treated' (p.131). If we expect prison officers to treat prisoners with the care and respect that creates hope which is a key component of desistance (Graham & McNeill, 2017), we must provide prison officers with the tools to create a rehabilitative culture (Karthaus et al., 2019). As I have outlined previously, within my role teaching prison officers, I have found that with all the determination in the world to make a difference, that cannot happen in isolation. Politicians and the public in the UK must ask what we want from the prison system. We cannot have rehabilitation on the cheap.

Researching health and well-being of prison officers Kinman et al., found that 'working conditions in the prison sector in the UK are far from satisfactory' (2016, p. 23). The public discourse must recognise, understand, and evaluate that these findings cannot be mutually exclusive to developing prisoners into positive community members. Prison officer well-being is undeniably, intrinsically linked to prisoner rehabilitation, public protection, and a reduction of victims. We need prisons that cultivate a culture of hope, not depend on isolated and enthusiastic officers such as several officers in these chapters to keep our communities safe. Let's have less unhelpful arguing about whether prisons should exist or not. They are here and we will continue to use them, so let's ensure all officers can be 'The Good Prison Officer' by setting the context for that to happen in every UK prison. We as a team present the following recommendations which align in some way with the Prisons Strategy White Paper (HMPPS, 2021) and what we believe would make a marked difference to our reoffending rates, from the *Inside Perspective*.

Recommendations from an Inside Perspective

1   All officers on the new apprenticeship scheme across the adult, women, and youth estate develop understanding of childhood experiences in the initial foundation training. How report after report finds disproportionalities of people of colour, care leavers and the school excluded within the prison system and how that should influence their relational practice. Max Dennehy, James Docherty and I have demonstrated that these roles are complex as found within literature presented in these chapters. The Foundation Training Programme on the current apprenticeship course stands

at 10 weeks (HMPPS, 2022b). We propose that a benchmark rather than duration for this initial training. We recommend that before new recruits start the next phase of the apprenticeships in their local prisons, they should meet set requirements for the use of force, communication, and a basic understanding of how adverse childhoods can influences health and social outcomes. We also believe as a team that the requirement of being 'at least 18 years old' (HMPPS, 2022a) is too young to be an officer. This should stand at 21 years old so that young people are not placed into what can be a traumatising role. The whole team feel that this role requires a level of maturity that many at 18 years of age simply do not have.

2   An offer of an on-the-job qualification for all prison officers at foundation degree level in criminology specific to the role of a prison officer like the MSc in Applied Custodial Leadership with the Unlocked Graduates Scheme in the adult estate. This will provide opportunities for grade 3 and 4 officers to educate themselves once they are in role and provide clear passages of progression, academically and professionally. HMPPS should attempt to make the role of the prison officer commensurate with Probation, Youth Justice, and Social Care to enable a culture of professionalism. However, this needs to be an applied degree given the nature of the role.

3   High quality clinical supervision must be standard practice within the role of a prison officer. At least one-hour clinical supervision per month by trained Custodial Managers, Psychologists, or other trained professionals to ensure any personal challenges are identified throughout the officer's career. This will likely positively impact on the poor retention rates which Max Dennehy and Charlie Taylor have outlined as a real issue for prisons (HMPPS, 2021). The Prisons Strategy White Paper states peer supervision will be introduced. This is a good start. However, we do not believe this goes far enough for a very complex role which exposes officers to primary and secondary trauma (Woodfield et al., 2019; Woodfield et al., 2022). Researchers exploring secondary trauma of correctional officers in the US for example have found that 'organizational practices, including role clarification, organizational support, and quality supervision, have been identified as protective factors' (Thomas, 2012, p. 30). If HMPPS want a rehabilitative culture, we must take care of officers that take care of prisoners and high-quality supervision for complex roles should be a standard they deserve. In June 2022, it was found that there is a complete lack of literature examining the supervision needs of prison officers. That if officers

receive emotional wellbeing training and supervision, it is likely 'to increase prison officer morale, reduce physical and mental ill health and lead to greater job satisfaction and retention of prison officers, ultimately, providing a more restorative and supportive prison environment' (Forsyth et al., 2022, para.38).

4 Transform Cat C prisons into open prisons so that many persistent and low-level people that offend can receive some level of normality while incarcerated. These individuals often require treatment programmes and detox facilities that are often not available in many communities in the UK. I went to prison twice to detox from heroin addiction. I would argue that this assisted me along my pathway to tertiary desistance. Having said that, had more treatment opportunities been available to me in the community, as well as other authors of this book, it is highly possible that some of the offending which resulted from the addiction would have not taken place. Where prison is the social response to such crimes, open prison would embed a principle of normality and allow such prisoners the opportunity to access employment, maintain family ties and prevent institutionalisation of people that are not *high* risk, but persistently causing social challenges because of the lack of social support services that meet their needs.

5 The apprenticeship scheme and any other training should include lived experienced trainers like the model delivered within the Unlocked Graduates masters. Youth Justice Workers (title of prison officers in the youth estate) working with incarcerated children are expected to obtain a level four qualification. This is good practice; however, the training doesn't seem to cover the topics the authors believe it should such as toxic stress, childhood trauma and lived experience realities of prison and social factors that drive offending. Increasing this training to a foundation degree for Youth Justice Workers including these topics would be in line with models such as Norway whereby 'education of POs has received accreditation as an academic degree programme' (Bruhn et al., 2017, p. 78). I have seen first-hand the benefits of educating the officers as well as practical learning from Unlocked Graduates and HMPPS. In the long run, the more Unlocked Graduates we have the in-prison system, the more innovative minds of officers are likely to create the change in culture that is required.

6 Introduce a lived experience leadership scheme within the HMPPS which has a kite mark that can be regulated and approved by an independent charity within the industry that advocates for lived experience. HMPPS are lacking behind third sector and charity

organisations offering opportunity for the likes of the authors of this book. This is unacceptable and we need to see more progressive thinking in this area. We recommend the development of leadership roles in all, including statutory, aspects of the justice system. This inclusion of different perspectives and influence in policy is likely to have a positive impact on changing the culture. Unlocked Graduates include lived experience expertise while the officers receive the two-year Masters. This level of inclusive training should be central to all officer training prior to employment. HMPPS should be leading the way in demonstrating their belief in desistance, not being left behind by charities and voluntary sector organisations such as the Prison Reform Trust (PRT), UserVoice, St Giles, Clinks, Criminal Justice Alliance (CJA) and others in employing and education lived experience.

7   Create a lived experience scholars programme launched by the HMPPS/MOJ which funds lived experience collaboration between leading scholars and those with personal experience of the prison system. This would need some consideration or research into the right individuals that can contribute as lived experience alone wouldn't qualify someone for this role. Having said that, this book is evidence that this value and insight can bring a lot to prison reform, programme evaluation, rehabilitation, and desistance scholarship. Scholars should be financially incentivised where possible to coproduce literature, research, and evidence alongside professionals with lived experience of prison, probation, and youth justice. There are calls for similar 'pipelines' of researchers with lived experience in mental health (Kimhy et al., 2022) – why not criminal justice.

8   Introduce better educational opportunities for serving prisoners. According to the Prison Strategy White Paper, there will be an introduction of a Prison Education Service to address the fact 'education provision is not good enough, with 60% of prisons in England receiving Ofsted grades of 'Requires Improvement' or 'Inadequate' over the last five years' (HMPPS, 2021, p.37). This is simply unacceptable after Coates (2017) highlighted that 42% of prisoners were permanently excluded from school in the review of prisoner education. DWRM is a company dedicated to improving prisoner access to higher education. Dan Whyte is the CEO of DWRM after serving a life sentence and is driven to support other prisoners to follow his footsteps onto a PhD. We would welcome more ex-prisoners being actively involved in supporting other prisoners to develop reading and writing skills required for employment upon leaving prison.

9   Following on from the last recommendation, I undertook a word search of the Prisons Strategy White Paper. I used the search terms peer–led, co-production, participation, and collaboration and found these terms were not used once in the entire document. These terms are fundamental to probation, youth justice, and prison practice. If these are to become a fabric of the justice institutions, politicians must understand their value and use such terms in public discourse. If we use these terms as well as punishment and rehabilitation, we demonstrate to the public that those that enter the justice system have skills that contribute to improving the justice system. Involvement of those skills in service design is a key element of justice service regulation frameworks (HMIP, 2019).

10 Creating a balanced and nuanced public discourse from politicians about reoffending is essential. Stating that prisoners must understand the 'consequences of failure to take responsibility for *their* rehabilitation' while the reoffending rate post custody stands at 42% within 12 months is loaded and misleading (HMPPS, 2021). There are scholars that argue 'prison is a part of a penal apparatuses that functions to reproduce itself' (Johns, 2017, p. 3). If prisoners have experienced abuse, trauma, addiction, racism, and poverty, as identified in the Prison Strategy White Paper, reintegration post custody surely cannot be placed solely at the feet of prisoners. Prison is an added adversity to lifelong challenges for many prisoners (Coates, 2017; Ford et al., 2019). The politicians responsible for macro policies that drive inequality, poverty and deprivation must *own* their role in the social phenomenon. Not just discuss micro level crime as if it happens in a vacuum. A slightly more nuanced discourse around the issue of crime and justice would go a long way to ensuring prisoners and ex-prisoners are not alienated from the employment market and defined as risks that need avoiding, but people that need additional support and inclusion because they bring skills (Henley, 2014).

11 The Prison Strategy White Paper states that the implementation of the Target Operational Model is to create a pathway for 'prisons and probation working seamlessly together as one service' (HMPPS, 2021, p.7). I have worked in youth justice for 15 years; this is different language outlining what is already done. Youth justice and probation have always worked closely with prisons because the practitioners supervise the prisoners risk levels while they are in custody and develop the prisoner's resettlement plans and licence conditions. The question raised here should be why it hasn't worked in the past. More research required instead of changing the

wording of a model. And who can we involve creating innovation. Kevin Neary's Aid&Abet is an organisation working with people on release from custody. This demonstrates the need for peer-led resettlement support and at least acknowledgment of the benefits of including such schemes upon release from custody.

12   Finally, we suggest two key principles or obsessions to aim towards. The first is an obsession for the governments in England and Wales, as well as Jersey, and Scotland to commit to reducing the prison population to pre 1990 numbers which stood at around 40,000 in England and Wales (Berman & Dar, 2013). The prison numbers have steadily increased due to successive Labour and Conservative governments assuring the British public that prisoners before the courts will be found prison places (see Ryan & Ward, 2015). This has been largely led 'by political decisions influenced, in part by inaccurate media (mis)representations and silences' (Mason, 2006, p. 252). We should focus more finances on preventing crime as opposed to responding to it in an unhealthy way and strive for a reduction in prison numbers as we have witnessed in Norway (Høidal, 2018). The second obsession is to ensure there is at least one officer for every two prisoners throughout the daily routine. Prison officers need the resources and autonomy to deliver effective interventions within the prison walls. Examining the features for the Strangeways prison riots, Boin & Rattray (2004) found that overworked and understaffed prison officers was a significant contributing factor. All the authors have made it clear that presence, attunement, connection and trusting relationships make a difference. If the obsession is to ensure prison officers are available relationally to create a rehabilitative culture, then that comes as a cost (Marzano & Adler, 2007). We appreciate these obsessions maybe seen as blue-sky thinking. However, we do believe a focus on obsessions can only be a good thing to aim for, whether achievable or not.

Breaking away from a cyclical life of crime and prison is a challenge in and of itself. Even more so for those that have served several prison sentences, those that have been in the care system, chronically addicted to drugs, excluded from school, and incarcerated as children. Therefore, I wanted to recognise and acknowledge the commitment, effort, and determination of all the authors for sharing their knowledge and wisdom in this collective effort to improve a justice system that needs it. It would be much easier to move on, walk away and forget about the label's *criminal, prisoner,* and *convict.* However, as with many people that desist from offending, this team of people have a calling to improve the system for the next generation. If you are a policy lead or academic and have taken the time to digest the contents of this book, you have demonstrated a focus to listen to everyone that has something to say on justice matters. So, you deserve a thank you too. I hope you enjoyed these *inside perspectives*.

References

Auty, K. M., Liebling, A., Schliehe, A., & Crewe, B. (2022). What is trauma-informed practice? Towards operationalisation of the concept in two prisons for women. *Criminology & Criminal Justice*. https://doi.org/10.1177/17488958221094980.

Berman, G., & Dar, A. (2013). *Prison population statistics*. House of Commons Library.

Boin, A., & Rattray, W. A. (2004). Understanding prison riots: Towards a threshold theory. Punishment & Society, 6(1), 47–65.

Bruhn, A., Nylander, P., & Johnsen, B. (2017). From prison guards to… what? Occupational development of prison officers in Sweden and Norway. *Journal of Scandinavian Studies in Criminology and Crime Prevention*, *18*(1), 68–83.

Bhuller, M., Dahl, G. B., Løken, K. V., & Mogstad, M. (2020). Incarceration, recidivism, and employment. Journal of Political Economy, 128(4), 1269–1324.

Case, S., & Haines, K. (2021). Abolishing youth justice systems: Children first, offenders nowhere. *Youth Justice*, *21*(1), 3–17.

Coates, S. (2017). Unlocking potential: A review of prisoner education. Ministry of Justice.

Crewe, B. (2011). Soft power in prison: Implications for staff–prisoner relationships, liberty and legitimacy. *European Journal of Criminology*, *8*(6), 455–468.

Cullen, F. T., & Gendreau, P. (2019). From nothing works to what works: Changing professional ideology in the 21st century. In *Clinical forensic psychology and law* (pp. 231–256). Routledge.

Day, A. M. (2022). Disabling and criminalising systems? Understanding the experiences and challenges facing incarcerated, neurodivergent children in the education and youth justice systems in England. *Forensic Science International: Mind and Law*, *3*, 100102.

Ford, K., Barton, E., Newbury, A., Hughes, K., Bezeczky, Z., Roderick, J., & Bellis, M. (2019). Understanding the prevalence of adverse childhood experiences (ACEs) in a male offender population in Wales: The prisoner ACE survey. Public Health Wales; Bangor University, Wrexham.

Forsyth, J., Shaw, J., & Shepherd, A. (2022). The support and supervision needs of prison officers working within prison environments. An empty systematic review. *The Journal of Forensic Psychiatry & Psychology*, 1–16.

Graham, H., & McNeill, F. (2017). Desistance: Envisioning futures. In P. Carlen, L. Ayres França (Eds), *Alternative criminologies* (pp. 433–451). Routledge.

Henley, A. (2014). Abolishing the stigma of punishments served: Andrew Henley argues that those who have been punished should be free from future discrimination. *Criminal Justice Matters*, *97*(1), 22–23.

Her Majesties Prison and Probation Service (2021), Prisons Strategy White Paper, Available on – Prisons Strategy White Paper – GOV.UK. Retrieved 17 July 2022, from www.gov.uk

Her Majesties Prison and Probation Service (HMPPS) (2022a). Becoming a Prison Officer. Available on – Become a prison officer | HM Prison & Probation Service. Retrieved 17 July 2022, from prisonandprobationjobs.gov.uk

Her Majesties Prison and Probation Service (HMPPS) (2022b). Prison Officer Apprenticeships Available on – Prison officer apprenticeships | HM Prison & Probation Service. Retrieved 17 July 2022, from prisonandprobationjobs.gov.uk

HMI Probation (2019). Service user involvement in the review and improvement of probation services. HMI Probation.

Høidal, A. (2018). Normality behind the walls: Examples from Halden Prison. *Federal Sentencing Reporter, 31*(1), 58–66.

Inside Time. (2022). Chief Inspector warns on prison officer shortage. *Inside Time the National Newspaper for Prisoners and Detainees.* Available on – [Chief Inspector warns on prison officer shortage – insidetime & insideinformation]. Retrieved 17 July 2022.

Johns, D. F. (2017). *Being and becoming an ex-prisoner.* Routledge.

Johnsen, B., Granheim, P. K., & Helgesen, J. (2011). Exceptional prison conditions and the quality of prison life: Prison size and prison culture in Norwegian closed prisons. *European Journal of Criminology, 8*(6), 515–529.

Karthaus, R., Block, L., & Hu, A. (2019). Redesigning prison: The architecture and ethics of rehabilitation. *The Journal of Architecture, 24*(2), 193–222.

Kimhy, D., Jones, N., & Dixon, L. (2022). Investing in a research workforce with personal experience of serious mental illness. Published online August 03, *JAMA Psychiatry.* doi: 10.1001/jamapsychiatry.2022.2026.

Kinman, G., Clements, A. J., & Hart, J. (2016). Work-related wellbeing in UK prison officers: A benchmarking approach. *International Journal of Workplace Health Management, 9*(3), 290–307.

Kinman, G., Clements, A. J., & Hart, J. (2019). When are you coming back? Presenteeism in UK prison officers. *The Prison Journal, 99*(3), 363–383.

Labutta, E. (2016). The prisoner as one of us: Norwegian Wisdom for American Penal practice. *Emory Int'l L. Rev, 31,* 329.

Liebling, A., Price, D., & Elliott, C. (1999). Appreciative inquiry and relationships in prison. Punishment & Society, 1(1), 71–98.

Lovell, B., & Brown, R. (2017). Burnout in UK prison officers: The role of personality. *The Prison Journal, 97*(6), 713–728.

Martinson, R. (1974). What works? – Questions and answers about prison reform. *The Public Interest, 35,* 22–54.

Mason, P. (2006). Lies, distortion and what doesn't work: Monitoring prison stories in the British media. *Crime, Media, Culture, 2*(3), 251–267.

Marzano, L., & Adler, J. R. (2007). Supporting staff working with prisoners who self-harm: A survey of support services for staff dealing with self-harm in prisons in England and Wales. *International Journal of Prisoner Health, 3*(4), 268–282.

Mjåland, K., Laursen, J., Schliehe, A., & Larmour, S. (2022). Contrasts in freedom: Comparing the experiences of imprisonment in open and closed prisons in England and Wales and Norway. *European Journal of Criminology, 0(0)*. https://doi.org/10.1177/14773708211065905

Prison Reform Trust. (2022). New figures reveal exodus of prison staff. Retrieved 17 July 2022, from https://prisonreformtrust.org.uk/new-figures-reveal-exodus-of-prison-staff.

Ryan, M., & Ward, T. (2015). Prison abolition in the UK: They dare not speak its name? *Social Justice, 41*(3 (137), 107–119.

Shammas, V. L. (2014). The pains of freedom: Assessing the ambiguity of Scandinavian Penal exceptionalism on Norway's prison island. *Punishment & Society, 16*(1), 104–123.

Tait, S. (2011). A typology of prison officer approaches to care. *European Journal of Criminology, 8*(6), 440–454.

Thomas, B. Jr (2012). 'Predictors of Vicarious Trauma and Secondary Traumatic Stress Among Correctional Officers.' *PCOM Psychology Dissertations.* 228. https://digitalcommons.pcom.edu/psychology_dissertations/228

Turner, M., & Peacock, M. (2017). Palliative care in UK prisons: Practical and emotional challenges for staff and fellow prisoners. *Journal of Correctional Health Care, 23*(1), 56–65.

Ugelvik, T. (2016). Prisons as welfare institutions?: Punishment and the Nordic model. In Y. Jewkes, B. Crewe, J. Bennett (Eds), Handbook on prisons (pp. 388–402). Routledge.

Woodfield, R., Boduszek, D., & Willmott, D. (2019). Introduction and psychometric validation of the prison personnel trauma measure (PPTM). *European Journal of Trauma & Dissociation, 3*(4), 257–262.

Woodfield, R., Boduszek, D., & Willmott, D. (2022). Latent profiles of PTSD, anxiety and depression and association with trauma exposure within prison personnel. *European Journal of Trauma & Dissociation, 6*(3), 100268.

De Viggiani, N. (2007). Unhealthy prisons: exploring structural determinants of prison health. *Sociology of Health & Illness, 29*(1), 115–135.

Youth Custody Service (YCS) (2020). Training and benefits, [Youth custody training, youth justice degree|HM Prison & Probation Service. Retrieved 17 July 2022, from prisonandprobationjobs.gov.uk

Afterword

A prison officer invariably comes face to face with everything they've been taught to despise – not only on a societal level but within themself. With this destructive mental construct in place, we must turn things on their side and become conscious, we must overcome our own beliefs in order to transition from a prison officer to a good prison officer.

Prisons have the opportunity and, according to the evidence provided in these chapters, the obligation to intervene in the chaotic, dysfunctional, and traumatic life of a person whose journey has gone awry. Committing crimes, acting out, depression, anxiety, addiction, and antisocial behaviour are all signals that the brain is not getting the fundamental nurturing and attention a potentially pro-social creature craves and needs.

A good prison officer understands that their role is about public and prison safety. This comes about by helping the prison resident regulate and stabilize by learning techniques to de-escalate, soothe, encourage, and guide, similar to what a parent does for a child. I would argue that the good prison officer is essentially reparenting those who commit crimes, as evidenced in the prison officers described in this book:

Andi Brierley talked reverently about one of the 'Gym Screws' who saw his 'turnaround story' which gave him a positive spin to his prison experiences. This helped Andi to see his own value.

Kevin Neary had the experience with Officer Mark who encouraged him to take classes, believing in him – showing Kevin he had potential and value. 'Always encourage anyone's dream because I am proof that it is possible.'

Max Dennehy described the subtleties of a good prison officer, knowing when to "selectively underenforce and when not to." Similar to a parent, a good prison officer must trust and walk the tightrope of letting a prison resident test the boundaries of life and make sure he isn't taking advantage of their good graces. These are also tests of trust and instinctively understanding of basic human needs.

Kierra Myles was guided by her Prison Officer who was kind and 'always offering support and asking her if [she] needed anything.' This helped create a sense of safety and allowed Kierra's nervous system to relax. This prison officer also advocated for Kierra, taking her out of harm's way from an abusive prison officer, similar to what a protective parent would do for their child.

Daniel Whyte's prison officer took the time to ask him: 'What are you gonna do for the next 17 or so years?' Encouraging him by saying 'If you exercise your body and mind, you will get through anything.' This helped reinforce Daniel's sense of self and helped him envision a future (which is a prefrontal cortex activity – evidence of being regulated).

Devon Ferns' first interaction with an officer showed him some of them 'do care' and he was able to develop strong relationships with several prison officers who 'went above and beyond' to show Devon he had a future. Again, helping create a sense of safety, community, and ability to plan for the future.

James Docherty still remembers the officer who asked him: 'What are you doing in here wee man, you're too good looking to be in here.'

In all these recollections, former prison residents were seen for their untapped possibility, for their humanity, for their sacredness. In essence, these officers were repairing the deficit of connection and love that was missing during childhood, helping their brains to heal. The American Psychiatrist and Senior Fellow of the Childhood Trauma Academy Dr. Bruce Perry explain that we do not have the capacity as humans to develop love and empathy in isolation. It is only through experiencing the action of loving and being loved that we develop these neural networks because our brains learn through experience (Perry & Szalavitz, 2007). The evidence within these chapters demonstrate that these actions can and need to unfold within the complex sphere of incarceration.

Further, those officers were able to see these residents' humanity because they were able to see their own. As James Docherty so eloquently says 'prison is about the loss of liberty, it should never be a loss of humanity.'

Prisons can create good criminals or good neighbours. A good prison officer is a key to helping create regulated, empathetic, caring, prosocial members of society with the added benefit of less stress, better life outcomes and a rewarding job. Creating this relational sphere within the carceral space is the very essence of this important text.

Fritzi Horstman, Founder of the Compassion Prison Project.

Reference

Perry, B., & Szalavitz, M. (2007). The Boy Who Was Raised as a Dog: And Other Stories from a Child Psychiatrist's Notebook Child Psychiatrist's Notebook – What Traumatized Children Can Teach Us About Loss, Love, and Healing.

Index

Notes: *Italicised* folios refers figures in the text.